DESIGN FOR CHRISTIAN LIVING

DESIGN FOR CHRISTIAN LIVING

SERMONS BY HUGH THOMSON KERR

Edited by

DONALD CRAIG KERR

Philadelphia

THE WESTMINSTER PRESS

Library of Congress Catalog Card Number: 52–11757

PRINTED IN THE UNITED STATES OF AMERICA

Acknowledgments

Nearly all the sermons used in this book have appeared in print at various times and through a variety of ways. The sermon entitled "What Memorial Have You?" was issued in abbreviated form by the Restoration Fund on behalf of the Presbyterian Church, U.S.A. A wider circulation was likewise given to the sermon on "What Protestant Christians Believe" when it was printed and distributed by the former Federal Council of the Churches of Christ in America. I wish to express my appreciation to the Council of Churches of Allegheny County and the Shadyside Presbyterian Church for their gracious consent in allowing the use in this book of material that they have had printed. It may be that some of these sermons have found their way into print through other means of which I do not know. If this be so, I can only attest to the fact that as far as I am aware I have followed the language and thought of the author as they were originally given by him.

I gratefully acknowledge permission given by the following individual and publishers to quote material used in this book:

Dr. Thomas Curtis Clark, for permission to use the poems "The Song of a Heathen," by Richard Watson Gilder, and "Light," by Francis William Bourdillon, from *One Thousand Quotable Poems,* edited by Thomas Clark and Esther Gillespie (Harper & Brothers); Doubleday and Company, for use of "The Explorer," from *The Five Nations,* by Rudyard Kipling, copyright, 1903, by Rudyard Kipling, and reprinted by permission of Mrs. George Bambridge and Doubleday and Company, Inc.; Charles Scribner's Sons, for permission to quote from "School Days," by Maltbie D. Babcock, in *Thoughts for Everyday Living.*

To One Whose Name
Is Seldom Mentioned
but
Whose Love and Care
Were Never Absent —
MY MOTHER

Contents

Foreword 9

A Brief Biographical Sketch 13

Section One

THE CHRISTIAN YEAR 17

1. The Fullness of Time 19
2. " The World's Most Beautiful Story " 22
3. King for a Day 26
4. " He Is Risen " 29
5. The Holy Spirit 32

Section Two

THE CHRISTIAN WORLD 37

6. How to Make the Old New 39
7. " The Crown Wherewith His Mother Crowned Him" 42
8. What Has War Taught Us? 47
9. A Day for Hope 51
10. The Sin of Thanklessness 55

Section Three

THE CHRISTIAN FAITH 59

11. The Christian Way to Think About God 61
12. The Christian Way to Think About Jesus Christ 66
13. The Christian Way to Think About Man 69
14. The Christian Way to Think About Faith 73
15. The Christian Way to Think About Forgiveness 77
16. The Christian Way to Think About the Life to Come 81

Section Four

THE CHRISTIAN LIFE 85
17. How to Be a Christian 87
18. How to Pray as a Christian 90
19. How to Suffer as a Christian 94
20. How to Endure Temptation as a Christian 98
21. How to Be Content as a Christian 101

Section Five

THE CHRISTIAN SERVICE 105
22. Christian and Pagan Ideologies 107
23. The Greatest Need of America 112
24. The Prince of Peace 115
25. The Only Way Out of the Dark 119
26. "The Mountain Shall Be Thine" 123
27. Christ — the Hope of the World 127

Section Six

THE CHRISTIAN CHURCH 131
28. The Church 133
29. The Gospel 138
30. What Protestant Christians Believe 142
31. What Memorial Have You? 147
32. The Foreign Mission of the Church 152

Foreword

It is not an easy matter to pick and choose among several thousand sermons, nor is the burden eased by virtue of the fact that a son is trying to show what was his father's best. Fortunately, a natural plan of procedure presented itself whereby it was possible to secure a limited but comprehensive selection. Following his retirement and for two or three years prior to his death, my father carried on a useful ministry in Pittsburgh by means of a regular Sunday morning radio service which he conducted on behalf of The Council of Churches of Allegheny County. Many of the sermons included in this book were a part of that radio ministry.

Radio preaching possesses a double virture: It must conform to certain prescribed limits of time, and its thought must be carefully worded. For that reason these sermons are both brief and concise. In presenting the central truths of our Christian faith and life, they offer to the clergy as well as to the laity a reinterpretation of that " old, old story " that we have " loved so long." With the Scriptures as their guide, they tell us, what Augustine long ago proclaimed, that " the heart of man is restless until it finds its rest in Thee." From out of the far-distant past the living Christ is brought into the present and made the light by which we travel in the pilgrimage of faith.

The contents of the book have been arranged under six headings, each representing some major emphasis in the practice of the gospel. It seems proper, therefore, that Section One should be devoted to the ancient and historic landmarks of our Christian heritage. As one sets out in search of a living faith, it is inevitable that certain high peaks of experience will begin to show themselves above the horizon. For the Christian these visual reminders are crystallized in the several intimate events related to our Lord's life, from which the essence of the gospel takes its meaning. The significance of this fact is made obvious as we follow the important themes of "The Christian Year," which is the general subject of the first section.

Section Two also deals with certain important events, which if they do not belong to the Christian year, are a part of the world in which we live. In every year there are dates on the calendar that denote some civic or patriotic observance. While such occasions do not necessarily bear a Christian identity, they do have a natural and cultural importance. Willing to be a champion for the supremacy of Christ in all things, the Christian is always ready to make the most of every opportunity; and thus finds a place for His gospel in politics, economics, the family, or the home. In all these things there is an inherent religious quality which needs to be made known. The sermons of the second section have therefore to do with these various aspects of "The Christian World."

In Section Three a series of six sermons has been arranged that speak directly to some of the simple but profound realities of "The Christian Faith." The need for an adequate expression of what we believe demands a constant clarification and review of the New Testament teaching. A pilgrim in his quest does not travel far before he wants to know more about God, about Jesus, about man, about faith, about forgiveness, about the life to come. While these articles of belief belong at one time or another to every sermon, they are treated in a specific doctrinal and expositional manner in the third section.

The problem of our time has to do with the interpretation of the gospel not only to the church and to those who worship there, but also, or more so, to the world outside the church. Since our natural association is with the world we know and the people who cross our daily path, we have to learn the secret of living with "all sorts and conditions of men." While it is good to withdraw for a season from the traffic of the day, we are by necessity thrown against the dreams, the failures, the sufferings, and the temptations of the world. In all the common duties of life there is never a decision that does not open the door to a Christian point of view. To relate Christ and his Church to the world around us is the desire of every disciple. The sermons in Section Four are thus concerned with those familiar interests and issues related to "The Christian Life."

Somewhere in his writings the German mystic Meister Eckhart remarked that there were always some who would follow Christ halfway, but there were not many who would follow the other half. Thus it becomes increasingly important to show the application and relevancy of the Christian's duty. In the pursuit of Christian values and in giving expression to a wholesome Christian life, we are immediately challenged by certain inescapable issues. We want to know, for example, wherein the gospel of Christ is in conflict with modern pagan ideologies. We want to be told what the heritage of America means. We want to know about the high cost of peace. We want to be sure about the integrity of the Bible. We want to speak to the idealism of youth. We want to be assured that Christ is the hope of the world. These are the particular questions which are considered in the fifth section, whose general heading is "The Christian Service."

If there is frequent reference in this book to the church, that is only natural. It is what we would expect. The church is the Christian's home. The church is the preacher's pulpit. It is the treasury of all that is highest and best within the long centuries of our Christian tradition. It is therefore altogether fitting that Section Six of this volume should have as its theme "The Christian Church." At a time in history when the world is pulling apart it is reassuring to know that the peoples of the earth can find their unity under the banner of the Church of Christ. The day is long past for the abolition of the word "sectarian" and for the fulfillment of our Lord's own words: "That they all may be one; as thou, Father, art in me, and I in thee, that they also may be one in us: that the world may believe that thou hast sent me." Upon this prophetic and triumphant call, so strong and clear, the challenge of the Church must rest, and from out of our response lies the dawn of a new tomorrow.

With a feeling of deep gratitude for this opportunity to present the record of a preaching ministry whose one desire was to interpret the will of God for the ways of man, I am happy to make known once more the name of Hugh Thomson Kerr and to acknowledge with pride the fact that a father's influence still prevails over his children. It is likewise a privilege to add to the already long list of my father's writings this other volume, the substance of which is from his hand and heart. From these pages may a blessing come that will quicken life and spirit in the continued pilgrimage of faith.

DONALD CRAIG KERR.

Roland Park Presbyterian Church
Baltimore, Maryland

A Brief Biographical Sketch

FOR the nearly eighty years of my father's life, his home and kindred were divided between two countries, Canada and the United States. For more than half a century Hugh Thomson Kerr was an American citizen. He was proud of his adopted country. He recalled its history and its original charter with affection and a deep sense of satisfaction. At the outbreak of the First World War his loyalty took him to the side of the troops overseas, where he served his country by working under the auspices of the Young Men's Christian Association.

However, the beginnings of my father's life were nurtured, not in the United States, but in Canada. His father and mother came to Canada from Scotland in 1858 and settled in the little town of Elora, Ontario, where Hugh Thomson Kerr was born on February 11, 1871, the seventh son of ten children, all of whom later entered professional life as physicians, dentists, attorneys, or ministers.

From a background of farming life, where there was little luxury but great faith, my father entered the University of Toronto. At the age of twenty-three he received his B.A. degree, and in the following year, his M.A. degree. Having signified his desire to study for the ministry, he registered at Knox College in Toronto, the theological school of the Presbyterian Church in Canada. One of the prerequisites of the theological training was that a student should serve as a missionary in some undeveloped region not too far away from the city. Fifty-five years ago there lay to the north of Toronto, 135 miles away, just such a region known as Muskoka. It was while my father was in this area one summer that he met by chance (or perhaps by Providence) a man from Pittsburgh, who, being of persuasive powers, influenced the young student missionary to come to Pittsburgh and enter the Western Theological Seminary there. This was done and graduation completed at the seminary by the year 1897. Ordination into the gospel ministry immediately followed, being administered at the hands of the Presbytery of Pittsburgh.

My father continued to live in Pittsburgh, and for four years was pastor of the Oakland Presbyterian Church, where some forty-five years later his youngest son was to preach his first sermon. In 1901 my father married Olive May Boggs, of Harmony, Pa. Soon after their marriage my father and mother left Pittsburgh for Kansas, where for six years their home was within the shelter of the First Presbyterian Church in Hutchinson. In 1907 the family moved to Chicago and for another six years father was pastor of the Fullerton Avenue Presbyterian Church. During this time he also held a position at the McCormick Theological Seminary as lecturer in systematic theology and religious pedagogy. In 1913 a call came from the Shadyside Presbyterian Church in Pittsburgh, and the family moved back home. Included now as two very important members of the family were my sister, Mrs. John Watson Harmeier, whose home is still Pittsburgh; and my brother, Dr. Hugh Thomson Kerr, Jr., Professor of Theology at Princeton Seminary. For thirty-three years father continued as pastor of the Shadyside Church, and for four years prior to his death he was its pastor-emeritus.

Preaching, teaching, writing — this was my father's threefold rule of faith and practice. More than once he traveled the length and breadth of the United States, crossing many times into Canada, preaching as he went. For fifteen years he served as president of the Board of Christian Education, and in 1930 he was elected Moderator of the General Assembly of the Presbyterian Church, U.S.A. By virtue of these important offices he was able to carry his preaching mission as far as duty and strength would permit.

In my father's life preaching and teaching were like inseparable friends. During his ministry in the Shadyside Church it was a weekly practice for him to meet and teach two groups of students. The one group was composed of students from the Carnegie Institute of Technology; the other, of students from the University of Pittsburgh. The teaching ministry was a vital part of his life, and in his closing years he held a position at Western Theological Seminary as lecturer in homiletics and worship.

Books, papers, pen, and pencil were the necessary tools of my father's study. They were as a means of grace for the interpretation of God's truth, and during the course of a lifetime some twenty books could be credited to his name as author. Two of these were the product of two lectureships. A *God-centered Faith* came from the Stone Lectures at Princeton Seminary. *Preaching in the Early Church* was the published volume of the Moore Lectures at San Francisco Seminary. For many years he was busily engaged in writing Sunday school lessons or in preparing material for use in A *Year with the Bible*, a daily Bible guide which has had continuous circulation for the past thirty-eight years. And where his name is not known in any other way people around the world are familiar with his half dozen or more children's story-sermon books.

One summer after the Second World War, he was commissioned to fly to Europe, as a representative of The Board of Foreign Missions of the Presbyterian Church, U.S.A., in conjunction with the World Council of Churches, to visit the waste places of war's aftermath. At the age of seventy-five he was flying across the ocean in an Army bomber, and for an entire year he gave himself to the task of raising $27,000,000 for the Restoration Fund of the Church. Another commission that gave him delight was his time of service as chairman of the committee that prepared The Book of Common Worship. Out of this study there came from his pen a book on *The Christian Sacraments*. Another joy in his ministry was the Radio Vesper Service, which for a quarter of a century was broadcast from the Shadyside Church on Sunday afternoons, sending the gospel as far as the North Pole and even into the antarctic. He also rejoiced in the fact that hundreds and thousands and even millions of dollars could be attracted and used in the name of the Church. From one of these bequests there originated the Pitcairn-Crabbe Foundation, for which my father acted as executive secretary for the last four or five years of his life.

His was a full and happy life. He had his honors and his awards. His was a simple faith born of honesty, integrity, work, and trust. On June 27, 1950, he died, and the funeral service was held in the place dearest to his heart, the Shadyside Presbyterian Church.

> "God of the past, our times are in Thy hand;
> With us abide.
> Lead us by faith to hope's true Promised Land;
> Be Thou our guide.
> With Thee to bless, the darkness shines as light,
> And faith's fair vision changes into sight."

—Second stanza of the hymn "God of Our Life," by Hugh Thomson Kerr.

DONALD CRAIG KERR.

Section One

THE CHRISTIAN YEAR

1

The Fullness of Time

[AN ADVENT SERMON]

"But when the fulness of the time was come, God sent forth his Son." — Gal. 4:4.

THE universe runs on scheduled time. The timepiece of the ages is never late. Scientists travel over sea and land thousands of miles to meet an engagement with the sun that is to be in eclipse. The scientist may be late but the universe — never. When the last minute ticks, sun and moon, stars and planets cross time's appointed boundary line. Through the ages one increasing purpose runs, and when the hour strikes God in his glory appears.

This is the Bible way of interpreting history. The apostle Paul expresses it in an unforgettable phrase. Speaking of the coming of Christ into human history, he said, "When the fulness of the time was come, God sent forth his Son." When the hand of the clock pointed to the hour, the bells of Bethlehem began to ring. When time had traveled to its zenith, the Word of God became flesh and dwelt with men.

The first thing to note is that the world was a unity. The Roman Empire stretched from Germany in the north to the coast of Africa in the south — two thousand miles; and from Britain in the west to Babylon in the east — three thousand miles. Wherever the tides moved they washed the shores of a land where Rome held sway, and Rome kept the peace of the world, and peace was essential for the proclamation of the gospel. Milton speaks of the fact that when Christ was born, "No war, or battle's sound Was heard the world around."

The second thing to note is that Rome made the world a neighborhood. Her ships made paths through the seas, and across the nations she built her famous roads that ran to the ends of the earth. Over these roads passed the commerce and culture of the world and across them, when the fullness of time came, passed the messengers of the gospel.

A third thing to note is that Rome was tolerant of all religions. Indeed, Rome cared little or nothing about religion. Had the intolerance of a later age existed — the intolerance of Nero and Domitian — Christianity might never have had a chance. But in the age of Augustus Christians were permitted to go everywhere preaching the gospel.

A fourth and most important thing to note is that the barrier of language had broken down. When the fullness of time came, the people of the world were on speaking terms with one another. Alexander the Great, all unconscious of the role he was playing, made that certain. He unified the Greek-speaking world, introduced Grecian culture to the East, and made Greek the language not only of Athens and Rome but of Antioch and Alexandria. The result is that our New Testament is written in the language of the market places of the world. Language became a vehicle for a preparation of the world for the gospel.

A fifth thing to remember is that when the fullness of time came, the religions of the world were bankrupt. The ashes on the altars of Rome and Greece were cold. The fires of faith had died down. In Rome the Pantheon was open to any human god who sought a place. In Greece one could find an altar erected to an "Unknown God." In Palestine the last of the prophets was crying in the wilderness. Morally and spiritually the world was bankrupt. Then the hour struck; the trumpet sounded; the curtain was lifted. The fullness of time came, and God sent forth his Son.

If we had eyes to see and ears to hear and hearts to understand what is going on all about us; if we had the vision, the imagination, the insight of a prophet, we would see that we too, in our day, are again at the fullness of time. What are the signs that the hour is again about to strike? What is the evidence? Certainly there is a striking parallel between what Paul called the fullness of time and our own age.

For one thing, the world today is striving for a unity that parallels the condition of the world before the coming of Christ. The tides of truth and error are washing the shores of every land

and of every nation. The ideas that are stirring the students of America are being introduced in the classrooms of Japan, India, and Africa. The highways of the air are free for the thought of the world. The markets of Japan and Australia rise and fall with the markets of Europe and America. The same music thrills audiences that assemble on sea and land around the world.

In the second place, before the coming of Christ, a universal language provided a medium of exchange. The great evangelical ideas of the gospel found in the prepared Greek language a vocabulary that could carry the gospel message. Have we today such a common language?

Some years ago Dr. Halsey, of The Board of Foreign Missions of the Presbyterian Church, U.S.A., published a little book entitled *The Seven Wonders of the Modern World*. One of these seven wonders of the modern world was the spread of the English language. Dr. Halsey wrote perhaps fifty years ago, and since then the marvelous spread of the English language is still more significant. One can travel the world over and never be out of touch with the sound of his native tongue. Through the literature and immigration of the people of the English-speaking world, the English language has become a medium of exchange between nations and even between the nationals of one nation who speak different dialects.

In the third place, when Christ came, the religions of the world were dead or decadent. Could there be any more striking parallel today? The ashes on the altars of the religions of the Orient are cold. It is either Christianity or it is nothing. It is Christianity or nihilism or atheism.

Robert Louis Stevenson has a few lines which he calls "The Celestial Surgeon." He is thinking of himself. He fears he is becoming indifferent to the highest spiritual realities. He fears that he is faltering in the great task of happiness. He fears that he is losing the morning face that becomes a man of the Spirit. He fears that he is accepting comfort and success without gratitude. And lest his spirit die, he cries out:

"Lord, . . .
Choose thou, before that spirit die,
A piercing pain, a killing sin,
And to my dead heart run them in!"

He prefers anything, any kind of celestial surgery, any pointed pleasure, any piercing pain, any overwhelming loss of fortune. He welcomes anything and everything that will keep his soul from being anesthetized by worldliness, from being lulled by luxury, coddled by comfort, silenced by selfishness.

The clock of history is again about to strike. The bells of Bethlehem are ready to ring. Again the voice of the prophet is heard in the land: "Awake, awake, put on thy strength . . . ; put on thy beautiful garments. . . . Shake thyself from the dust; arise, sit on thy throne [A.S.V.]." There is no time to lose. The issue is urgent. For you and for me, at least, the issue is urgent; for God's eternal timepiece will soon beat out for each of us its measured invitation and challenge. Let us be on watch for the coming of our Lord, that with his hand touching ours we may come together into his Kingdom of joy and peace and blessedness.

2

"*The World's Most Beautiful Story*"

[A CHRISTMAS SERMON]

"*Glory to God in the highest,*
And on earth peace,
Good will toward men." — Luke 2:14.

THE Gospel of Luke has been called the world's most beautiful book. If Luke is the most beautiful book in the world, then the Christmas story is the most beautiful story among all the beautiful stories in that most beautiful book. In every land, in every language that has been reduced to writing, every child knows that this is the story of Christmas.

The Bible is full of inimitable short stories, but of all the stories this is the best. If you wish to give immortality to literature, you must give your words wings. If you can wed your history to song or story, it will fly out into the world and will not rest until the tale is heard in every language. Here in this story history is wedded to music. There is no story like it. Little children love it; old folks listen to it with rapt attention.

Let us think first of the singers. The singers are the angels. They have come out of the invisible. They are heavenly choristers in God's great cathedral of nature. The clouds are their curtains. The stars are their tapers. We would never have thought of such a story. It is a story not of man's invention or discovery. It is a surprise. We would never have thought of it. It is inconceivable. The angels have come out of the invisible and stand on solid ground beside the shepherds who keep watch over their flocks. What does it mean? It means that heaven and earth are one. It means that the visible and the invisible, the seen and the unseen, belong to one world. It means that earth opens out into heaven and the angels and man belong in the family of God.

Scientists are never tired of telling us about the marvelous unity of the physical world. The spectroscope has revealed the fact that the most distant star that eye has ever seen is the same in substance with the infinitesimal atom that is invisible. So God would have us think of the larger world, the universe of life. It is one world. It is a house of many mansions—our Father's house; and God is in every minute of it. That is what the presence of the angels meant.

Let us think of the song. There are those who say that the story is a fairy tale, perhaps one of God's fairy tales. They suggest that the shepherds heard no music, that there were no angels, and perhaps no shepherds and no Christ-child. But the wonderful and incredible thing is that here is the song that was sung. We can read it. We can sing it. So strange and wonderful is the song that no singer we have ever known could have penned the words or composed the music. Certainly the shepherds could not have thought it out, and in that dead, decadent age there was no one who could have manufactured the meter and invented the thought.

What a song it is! The chorister, or herald angel, sings his recitative alone, on the ground beside the shepherds: "Fear not: for, behold, I bring you good tidings of great joy, which shall be to all people. For unto you is born this day in the city of David a Saviour, which is Christ the Lord." Then the heavenly chorus, made up of innumerable angelic choristers, take up the refrain which echoes through the night: "Glory to God in the highest, and on earth peace, good will toward men." It is all one song. The herald angel gives the theme, and the theme contains the Christmas message: "Unto you is born . . . a Saviour." That is the message that is given. That is the theme: "Unto you . . . a Saviour."

That is not what the world was looking for. That is not what the world wants. It wants an adviser, an orator, a scholar, a philosopher, a scientist, a philanthropist, a big-business man. But what the world needs is a Saviour. For sin is here and fear is here and sometimes the night is dark and there are no stars. This is the most glorious message that was ever sung in song or story: "Unto you is born . . . a Saviour."

I think I could have arranged it differently. I think I could have improved upon the scenery and the background. I would have arranged it, not out on the plains of Judea in the presence of a few scantily clad shepherds. I would have staged the Christmas pageant amid the glories of Herod's Temple on Mount Sinai in Jerusalem. I would have had the radiant heavenly light illumine the candlesticks and the altar and the golden bowls of the Temple. I would have arranged the angel choir so as to sing an antiphonal chorus, while the high priest and all the priests and the Levites and the great, crowded audience of wondering people bowed in silence as the music echoed from corridor to court. I would have had all Jerusalem thrill to the song of "Glory to God in the highest."

That is the way I would have done it. That is the way we would have arranged it, if we had had anything to do with this

Christmas pageantry. But that would not have been God's way. God's way is the Bible's way. God works in secret and in obscurity. He gives his revelation under cover of the night. He comes, not to priests and to kings, but to shepherds and to lowly folk. His voice is not heard in the street. God speaks within the loneliness of the hills.

> "How silently, how silently
> The wondrous gift is given!
> So God imparts to human hearts
> The blessings of His heaven."

This is what Christmas means. If Christmas means anything, it means that all life is filled with glory and melody and joy, and that fear has forever fled. In one of her remarkable utterances Jenny Lind, "the Swedish nightingale," summed up the high purpose of her life with these four words: "I sing for God."

So the shepherds went back to their task, each one holding his secret in his heart and saying to himself, "I keep sheep for God." That is the spirit that has transformed the world. "I do business for God." "I drive an automobile for God." "I plow fields and gather the harvest for God." "I practice medicine for God." "I nurse the sick for God." "I make money for God." "Glory to God in the highest." Anything I can do or say or sing I lay at his feet. I give him what I have, whether it be gold or frankincense or myrrh, whether it be my song or my sermon, my scholarship or my sheep over which I keep watch. "Glory to God in the highest."

3

King for a Day

[A PALM SUNDAY SERMON]

> "*Tell ye the daughter of Sion,*
> *Behold, thy King cometh unto thee,*
> *Meek, and sitting upon an ass,*
> *And a colt the foal of an ass.*" —Matt. 21:5.

FOR one day Jesus was crowned king. For one short day he was feted and garlanded and crowned. For one brief day the scepter was put into his hand. For one day, with no mockery in the cry, the people shouted, "Blessed is he that cometh in the name of the Lord; Hosanna in the highest." For one day the palms waved for him and the children sang. For one day he answered the question of the Wise Men, "Where is he that is born King?" For one short day he was king. Five days later, on Good Friday, he was crucified.

We speak of it as the "triumphal entry," but where was the triumph? The Romans knew what a triumphal entry was like. Pompey had entered Rome with a long retinue of captives from other lands following in his train like slaves. Tablets were carried through the crowd on which were inscribed the names of a thousand cities which he had conquered. For two days the vast procession passed with the waving banners and the sound of trumpets and the proclamation was made that Pompey was the emperor and conqueror of the whole world. There was a triumphal entry into Jerusalem when Kaiser Wilhelm entered the city through a new gate that had been opened in the wall for his approach.

But the world never saw anything like this. What does it mean? Here is Jesus, a carpenter, a peasant from far-off Galilee, riding into the city on a colt, going forward receiving the plaudits of the crowd, listening to the shouts of the populace: "Hosanna! Hosanna!" What a pageant it is! It is so unlike Jesus and yet it was of Jesus' own planning. He wanted to teach the people through their eyes what they were unwilling or unable to hear with their ears. He had been speaking to them about the cross and sacrifice, and they had turned a deaf ear to everything that he had said.

The day before, two of his disciples had asked to sit at the right hand of his power and he had said, "Whosoever will be great among you, let him be your minister; and whosoever will be chief among you, let him be your servant: even as the Son of man came not to be ministered unto, but to minister, and to give his life a ransom for many." But they were too blind and too dumb to understand. They could think only in political terms, and now he seeks to make them understand through this strange pageant that he is King, riding in triumph but not as a military conqueror, riding upon no war horse, with no soldiers, no trumpets, but riding upon an ass, the symbol of domesticity and peace, meek and lowly.

The triumphal entry suggests that when Christ is crowned King, the dreams and hopes of all the past are fulfilled. The people acknowledged him and gave him his real rights. The day before, he had said: "The princes of the Gentiles exercise dominion over them, and they that are great exercise authority upon them. But it shall not be so among you"; but they did not understand. How could they understand? They had lifted out of the Old Testament all the prophecies that spoke of royalty and rank and conquest; they had lifted out of the Old Testament all those words about a king reigning in righteousness, holding in his hand the scepter of authority, the mighty God, the King of Kings ruling the nations with a rod of iron; and now Jesus, who understood the Old Testament better than they did, is saying to them, "No! I am not that sort of king."

There was another strand of prophecy in the Old Testament that pointed out the true way of the Messiah. They had never thought of the Messiah in such terms. He was "despised and rejected of men; a man of sorrows, and acquainted with grief." They never thought of singing a hymn such as we sing, "The King of Love My Shepherd Is." Their minds were full of drums and trumpets and military victories, and Jesus is speaking to them of the triumph of meekness and lowliness and love. In other words he is saying, "Come unto me, all ye that labor and are heavy laden, and I will give you rest." We know well enough today that the type of kingship and leadership that Jesus proclaimed that day is the only real leadership.

Furthermore, when Christ is crowned King, there is the consecration of all possessions. "If any man say aught unto you, ye shall say, The Lord hath need of them; and straightway he will send them." When Christ is made King, all that we have and own is laid at his feet. When he needs the colt, the colt is turned over to him. He claims the canvas of the painter, the verses of the poet, the book of the writer, the song of the musician, the wealth of the rich man, the power of the politician. There is nothing in all the world that Christ does not claim, and that he does not get when he is crowned Lord of all.

We are told that John Bunyan turned a woman out of a church for wearing a silk dress, but Christ claims the silk and the satin and the beauty of all the world. It is said that Fra Angelico would paint only sacred subjects, but Christ claims all the paintings, demanding that all art be made subservient to his will. Frances Havergal would sing only sacred songs, but Christ claims all the music, and if his claim were recognized, there would be a sweetening and heightening of the musical tone of the world. Christ claims all our resources. He says to us, what he said to the disciples, "Bring them to me." There will be no begging and no deficits in the Christian Church when Christ is crowned.

And then, too, when Christ is crowned King, there is an outburst of spontaneous joy and enthusiasm. It ought to be that wherever Christ comes, joy breaks out. It was so in the Early Church. It was so even in the catacombs. Upon the soft chalk walls they drew the picture of Orpheus and his lyre, drawing the beasts and birds to him because of the sweetness of his music. It was so with Christ. When properly presented, he allures and attracts through his winsomeness and charm.

Life to most people is lived on a rather narrow margin. To most people life is hard and difficult. To many people there is the burden of loneliness and anxiety and care, and religion comes into life, not to add another burden, but to lift the load, to sweeten life, to create a new song. Don't have anything to do with a church or a religion or a creed that cannot be set to music. The greatest of all the Christian creeds is the "Te Deum Laudamus," which has sung itself through the Church down to our own day, lifting the note of triumphant gladness to the words: "We praise Thee, O God: we acknowledge Thee to be the Lord. All the earth doth worship Thee: the Father everlasting."

King for a day! That is the tragedy of the triumphal entry, but it need not be. He still rides through the world conquering and to conquer. He can come into our hearts and into our homes, and into our national and international life and when he comes, he will satisfy all our dreams and hopes, causing us to consecrate to him all that we are and have and setting our lives to the music that is the gladness of the world.

4

" He Is Risen "

[AN EASTER SERMON]

"And declared to be the Son of God with power, according to the Spirit of holiness, by the resurrection from the dead."
— Rom. 1:4.

We are here this morning because something happened in Jerusalem nineteen hundred years ago. We are here to repeat the message, "Christ is risen." It is the fact that comes first, for if Christ be not risen, this service is a sham, the Bible is a fiction, this music is a mockery. As was said long ago, if Christ be not risen, and the resurrection of Christ not a fact rooted in reality, then preaching is nonsense, faith is foolishness, our experience is false, our sins are unforgiven, and of all people in the world we are the most pitiable, because we are taking part in a scenario that has no relation to reality. We can only return to the ghostly shapes and shadowy forms of paganism.

It is well for us to look at the consequences of this tremendous fact apart from the thrill and romance of a modern Easter Sunday. We go back before there was any hymnal or any New Testament and look facts in the face. Let us hear what the most brilliant intellect of a generation after this event has to say. Saint Paul is writing to a little group of believers in the city of Rome, and he says that Jesus Christ our Lord was "declared to be the Son of God with power, according to the Spirit of holiness, by the resurrection from the dead." That statement contains three great affirmations.

First, the resurrection is the vindication of Jesus of Nazareth as the Son of God. He came among men as Jesus of Nazareth — carpenter, teacher, prophet, martyr. But that was not what he truly was. He lived as a peasant. He suffered poverty. He was despised. He was hounded by the authorities. He was crucified as a criminal. "This man," they said, "is not of God." "We know that this man is a sinner." Of him it was written, "He was in the world, and the world was made by him, and the world knew him not." He was in the world incognito.

One day in the city of Lucerne a tragic accident took place. An automobile leaped the curb, struck a tree, and fell into the lake. A young woman was killed. It was a sudden, shocking tragedy, and sympathy was everywhere expressed. Later, when it became known that the young woman was the queen of Belgium, a wave of emotion passed over the city. She had been traveling incognito and only her death disclosed her rank. The tragedy of her death revealed her royalty. It was something like this that happened in the life of Jesus. He died upon the cross, forsaken even by his friends. When the cross was lifted on Calvary there was not one Christian in the whole world. Then came the miracle of the resurrection and suddenly his own people awoke to the significance of who he was. In the mighty power of that great demonstration Jesus of Nazareth was vindicated as the Son of God. The fact of the resurrection declared him to be more than the son of

David according to the flesh. It declared him to be the Son of God, and it installed him, invested him, in power — even Jesus Christ our Lord — and for that reason we, and millions of Christians, have gathered to worship him this Easter Day.

Secondly, the resurrection is the vindication of his life as the Son of Man. The resurrection put its stamp upon his life, his morals, his ethics, his character, his teaching. If you want to know what sort of life is real and true and abiding, even as Pilate said, " Behold the man! " These are days when the changing moral standards of life are causing bewilderment on the part of serious-minded young people. Today we see how Christ's interpretation of life, his philosophy of the meaning of life, receives vindication. It is the last word that counts.

Did Pilate, with his moral cowardice, have the last word? He thought he had. Did Caiaphas, with his prejudice, have the last word? He thought he had. Did Herod, with his frivolity, have the last word? He thought he had. Did Judas have the last word? He thought he had. He betrayed him with a kiss. And Jesus let it all pass. He acted as much as to say, " Wait a little — today — and tomorrow — and tomorrow." It is the last word that counts and Jesus had the last word. What a tragedy it would be if we had to live in a world where the soldiers and the politicians and the Herods and the Pilates and the Judases and the Communists had the last word! What a ghastly world it would be! It would be a world where we should be compelled to accept the authority and domination and control of envy and hatred and prejudice and cowardice and avarice and frivolity and death. The resurrection of Jesus Christ puts an end to that bad dream. The old world died with Christ and a new world was born.

Thirdly, the resurrection is the revelation of what death really means. We know now how to interpret death. We know what lies yonder beyond the darkness. Here is the answer to all our questions about the life that lies beyond time. This is the pledge of the life that is to be. This is the assurance that life will not be emptied of those personal and intimate relationships which make life worth-while. When we pass from the life that we know to the life that lies beyond the shadows, we shall not be afraid or troubled; for we shall stand, as we stand now, in the presence of One whom having not seen we love.

Christ is our warrant that we shall see no longer through a glass darkly but face to face. He calls Mary by her own name. He meets Peter alone and heals the wounds of the past. He meets the disciples on their way to Emmaus and their hearts burn within them as he holds fellowship with them. In the upper room, as on the night before he was betrayed, he comes bringing peace. That is always his watchword. He comes, not to alarm, but to comfort. If the religion you have is a burden to you, if it leads to discouragement and fear, then you can be sure you do not have the religion of Jesus Christ. If your life is irritable and filled with controversy and vexed with suspicion, you may know full well it is not the Christian faith that you possess.

And that assurance he now gives. Immortality in the Christian sense belongs to the soul — now. " This is eternal life to know God and Jesus Christ whom he has sent." It is a quality of life. It is life in another dimension. It is life viewed, not on a horizontal plane, but in a vertical plane. It is life that comes down from above. " Therefore if any man be in Christ, he is a new creature: old things are passed away; behold, all things are become new." Hallelujah! Christ is risen!

5

The Holy Spirit

[PENTECOST]

" *And they were all filled with the Holy Ghost.*" — Acts 2:4.

AFTER his resurrection, Jesus told his disciples to wait for the promise of the Spirit; and on the Day of Pentecost this great miracle took place. The people who had not been touched by it were mystified and bewildered and spoke of those who had experienced it as being " full of new wine." But Peter said: " Ye men of Judea, and all ye that dwell at Jerusalem, be this known unto you, and hearken to my words: The prophet Joel long ago said, It shall come to pass in the last days, saith God, I will pour out my Spirit upon all flesh: and your sons and your daughters shall prophesy, and your young men shall see visions, and your old men shall dream dreams. And I will show wonders in heaven above, and signs in the earth beneath; blood, and fire, and vapor of smoke: the sun shall be turned into darkness, and the moon into blood, before that great and notable day of the Lord come: and it shall come to pass, that whosoever shall call on the name of the Lord shall be saved." " Now," says Peter, " this is that. This is the day of the Spirit. This is the outpouring of the Spirit of God upon all flesh. This is the new age, the new world, the new power of God." The stars did not fall. The sun was not turned into darkness. The moon was not turned into blood. There was no blood, or fire, or vapor of smoke. But this was it. This was the day of the Lord. This was the new world wherein dwells righteousness.

Whatever God, in his providence, has for this world of blood and iron, of clouds and thunder, of continents and oceans, of suns and stars and circling planets, let us be sure of this that the coming of Christ, the coming of the Spirit of God, was no passing thing, no result of necessary change, no outcome of evolution, but a world-transforming crisis in the life of humanity that destroyed the old world, that put to rout the flesh and the devil and established in our midst the Kingdom of God.

It belongs to us here and now to enter into this new order and this new life. God has done everything that he can do. He has given us the gospel. He has come near to us in Christ. He has through the cross condemned sin. By the resurrection he has brought in a new order. He has inaugurated, by the Spirit of Pentecost, the Church, the norm of a new society, the Beloved Community, the Kingdom of God, which is " righteousness, and peace, and joy in the Holy Ghost." To destroy this world in fire and flood would accomplish nothing. We must plunge headfirst into the Christian faith.

If what has been said about Pentecost is true, then light is shed upon the entire Christian faith. The coming of the Holy Spirit is the pledge that Christ and his salvation are made available for all men. They are no longer struggling up to God. God has come down to them. They are not alone. God is in them. They do not save themselves. God saves them by his Spirit.

The neglect of the work of the Spirit throws a man back upon himself. He tries to do what only God can do. He fails in faith and trust and consequently his religion becomes one of effort, whereas it is the Spirit of God who alone can make the work of Christ effectual. If the Spirit is ignored, we have nothing save our own inadequate endeavors.

The words of an eminent psychologist, Professor Hadfield, may be more revealing than words spoken by a theologian: "Looking at the Church of today, one cannot but be struck with its powerlessness. . . . This want of . . . power is associated with the fact that men no longer believe in the existence of the Spirit in any effective, practical way. They believe in God, the Father, and they are reverent; they believe in the Son, and the Church numbers amongst its members millions who humbly try to follow in his steps; but for all practical purposes they are like the little band at Ephesus who had 'not so much as heard whether there be any Holy Ghost,' and lacking the inspiration of such a belief, they are weak and wonder why." (From *The Psychology of Power*, J. A. Hadfield. The Macmillan Company, 1924.)

First of all, then, all that God is may be made available for us through the ministry of the Spirit. The Holy Spirit conveys God the Father to us. Emerson somewhere says that if a straw is laid parallel with the Gulf Stream, the Gulf Stream will flow through it. A human life may become the channel of divine life and power. Mr. Moody used to say: "Columbus discovered America; but what did he know about its great lakes, rivers, forests, and the Mississippi valley? He died without knowing much about what he had discovered. So, many of us discovered something of the love of God; but there are heights, depths, and lengths of it we do not know. That love is a great ocean; and we must plunge into it before we really know anything of it." We must plunge headlong into the Christian faith: "the day of the Lord" has come.

In the second place, all that Christ is for us and for our salvation is made available for us through the Spirit. The way in which the early Christians spoke of the Spirit is very striking. They thought of the presence of the Spirit as the presence of the living Christ. There was awakened within the hearts of the disciples the undying conviction that Jesus Christ was alive. Throughout the book of The Acts, the Holy Spirit is frequently identified with the living Christ. Pentecost was his coming again to the disciples. It was the verification of his promise. It was the fulfillment of his pledge. He had gone away that he might come again in power; and the New Testament bears evidence on every page that the early Christians felt that one like unto the Son of God was ever at their side. They went everywhere preaching that Jesus was alive. Their message was winged with the story of the resurrection. The note of certainty was in their word.

We are always ready to identify power with some force that is explosive. The New Testament identifies it with love. Love is the great power in the world. Love never fails. The fruit of the Spirit is love. God is love. Christ is love. That is why Christianity has the last word. It alone can conquer the hatred and the war spirit of the world. It alone can conquer the faithless and doubting human heart. The scientist George John Romanes came to the time and place where his faith failed. He said sadly but dispassionately, "There can no longer be any more doubt that the existence of a God is wholly unnecessary to explain any of the phenomena of the universe — no more doubt than if I let go of my pen it will fall upon the table." Before he died, after a deeper study of science and a still deeper understanding of life, he quoted the lines,

> "The mind has a thousand eyes,
> And the heart but one;
> Yet the light of a whole life dies,
> When love is done."
>
> — *From "Light," by Francis W. Bourdillon.*

Then he wrote his confession: "Love is known to be all this, how great then is Christianity as being the religion of love, and causing men to believe both in the cause of love's supremacy and that infinity of God's love to man."

There are great areas in life today that are not yet under the influence of the Spirit of Christ. These areas exist in every nation, in industry, in scholarship, in politics, and even in religion. It is written in the Gospels that Christ could do no mighty works in Galilee because of the unbelief of the people. There was no communicating channel for the divine influence. The power of God is as available for us as the power of nature. In the words of Dr. Rufus Jones: "The dynamo makes no electricity; it is a contrivance which lets electricity break through and do its work. The magnetic needle creates no magnetism. It merely lets vaster energies operate. That is what the broadcaster and transmitter of the telephone and the coherer of the wireless do. They all let energies break through and manifest themselves. The energy of nature is inexhaustible. There are those within and without the Church who seem to think that God is now exhausted, that the source of the new life of the Spirit has spent itself. How foolish! The conditions of spiritual life are still operative. 'Prove me now herewith, saith the Lord of hosts, if I will not open you the windows of heaven, and pour you out a blessing, that there shall not be room enough to receive it.'"

Section Two

THE CHRISTIAN WORLD

6

How to Make the Old New

[A NEW YEAR'S DAY SERMON]

"*When they saw the star, they rejoiced with exceeding great joy.*" — Matt. 2:10.

THE closing sentence of the story of the Wise Men is deeply significant. You remember that after the Wise Men from the East had followed the star and found the Christ-child, they were warned not to return to Herod; so they departed into their own country *another way*. It is this sentence that is arresting. What was the other way by which the Wise Men returned to their own country?

It is impossible for us to tell. It may have been a new road over the hill country or down the valleys, but it led them back to their own land with their wonderful new message. Certainly they returned to their own country with different hearts and a different outlook on life; for they returned with a new experience. They had come as seekers. They were going back as discoverers. They had come as astrologers. They were returning as Christians. That of itself would make the way home a different way. Those who drive automobiles know how the same road in the daylight is a vastly different road in the darkness; and these men went back again to the old scenes, the old home, the old work over a different road.

I would like to have you think about that. It is a good thing to come back to the old familiar places with a new hope in one's heart and a new spring in one's step and a new purpose in one's life, to come back to the old scenes over a new road. Mr. Gilbert K. Chesterton has said something on this subject, and said it in his usually arresting way. He said he would like, sometime to enter his home in a totally different way from what was his usual custom. He went on to suggest that he might get a ladder and enter like a burglar in the night, through one of the rear upper windows of his home; and so obtain a new thrill, a new experience, a new point of view of his own home. From this new point of view things would look different. We understand what Mr. Chesterton means. He is expressing the wish that he could have new eyes to see the meaning and value, and perhaps the defects, of the things that were most familiar to him. Whether it is over a different road made with hands or over a different highway made by a change of heart and a new mental outlook, certainly it is worth-while for us to try to redeem that which is old and familiar and to come into a new appreciation of the familiar.

It would be worth-while coming into our own homes over a different way. Perhaps familiarity has dulled our sense of appreciation. There is an old and true saying that the best thing about going away from home is coming home again. We know how it thrills us after vacation is over, or after an absence of weeks or months, to return to the old scenes. We enter, as it were, as Chesterton wished to do, through a new approach; and there is a glory about the old things — the pictures on the wall, the rugs on the floor, the dishes on the table, the books on the shelves. It would be well for some men who always enter through the front door to come in by the back door or up through the laundry and get some new sense of perspective as to household duties. It might be well for some of our hard-working mothers to come in through the front door, into the quiet, and look at things from a more restful and leisurely point of view.

It is told how Henry W. Grady, the eminent journalist to whom fame and position had come, slipped away from his office to his old home and to his mother, and entered his boyhood home seeking the renewal of his faith and hope and love in the presence of his mother. There is a remarkable story in the Gospel of Mark about a man who had been wonderfully cleansed and healed by Jesus, and out of gratitude this redeemed man besought the Lord to let him abide with him and follow him so that he might live in his fellowship. But Jesus said, "No, go back home and tell them what great things the Lord hath done for thee." One cannot help feeling that somehow there was a tragedy behind this man's story and our imagination follows him as we go with him in his cleansed and sweetened life back to the old home. What a glory there would be to thousands of homes if some young man or woman who has been living at cross-purposes would return through the door of a Christian faith to the old familiar scenes!

Perhaps, too, it would be worth-while to come into church by a different way. It is worth-while to try. At least, it is worth thinking about. Suppose we ministers who have been entering the church through the private or professional door of the pulpit should come into the worship and work of the church over another road. Instead of entering the church from the study and the pulpit and the cloister, suppose we come in through the front door with the worshipers, entering by way of the pew. It might make a difference. We might discover in that way that the world and religion look different from the point of view of the pew.

On the other hand, it would be like a revival in many churches for the members of the church to enter in by way of the pulpit. It would be a very profitable experience for the worshiper to enter in through the minister's study — say, at the close of the day, perhaps in the quiet of a Sunday evening — and think through with him the disappointments and failures and successes of the day that is gone.

Above everything else, I should like to discover some new way into the understanding and appreciation of the gospel of Christ. Probably we should all agree about that. We should like to enter into a deeper spiritual experience of his love and grace. Once in every twenty-five years the Sacred Portal of St. Peter's is opened and the pope, with his retinue of cardinals, enters into the great cathedral. They enter through that sacred door by a new way into the cathedral four times a century. Perhaps only once in a man's life would he be permitted to enter through that new and sacred passage. How different the cathedral would appear to them and what new and strange emotions would be awakened in their hearts! It is something like this that I should like to experience. I should like to enter the great cathedral of God's redeeming love through some hitherto unused gateway.

Lord Tennyson once said that his greatest desire in life was to have a fresh vision of God. That is what we all desire. We should like to have a new experience of God's reality. We should like to be taken up into the mountain and see Jesus transfigured. We should like to sit in the upper room and hear the rush of the Pentecostal wind. We long to stand in the garden — it may be beside a new-made grave — and hear the familiar voices speaking our name. There are countless folk today in this worldly and secular age who hunger and thirst for this deeper spiritual experience. They are praying, not for the opening sky or for an angel visitant, but for the removal of the dimness of their spiritual sight.

Can that prayer be answered? The New Testament says it can. The New Testament is all for fresher and deeper experiences. It is never tired of speaking of the inexhaustible resources and inexhaustible riches that are in Jesus Christ. It is always possible to know him better, but the path to that knowledge is the difficult path of discipleship. To all who would enter into a deeper experience of spiritual values, he says, "Follow me"; and that commands men following him not alone to the mount of transfiguration but down into the valley of humble service. Perhaps now in the new year the new vision of Christ will come to us through a closer following and a more consecrated service.

7

"The Crown Wherewith His Mother Crowned Him"

[A MOTHER'S DAY SERMON]

"Go forth, O ye daughters of Zion, and behold king Solomon
With the crown wherewith his mother crowned him."
— S. of Sol. 3:11.

ONE hesitates to use Mother's Day as a theme for preaching the gospel of Christ. The flower shops and the fruit shops, the candy shops, the telegraph and telephone have all cashed in on it. The lovely sentiment which it enshrines has been betrayed and one is tempted to pass the day by. But everything that is good and fine and wholesome is in danger of being commercialized. Christmas has been commercialized. There is danger that Easter will follow in the same path. Sunday has been commercialized. So it is good that we should pause and take note of what is right in days that in themselves are good.

One of the store windows in a big city displayed some time ago an advertisement which was a sermon on Mother's Day. In the window appeared the enlarged portraits of the mothers of fourteen of the great men of the world. The portraits of the mothers of McKinley, Coolidge, Taft, Dwight L. Moody, Abraham Lincoln, Napoleon, George V, Edward VII, Theodore Roosevelt, and Thomas Edison, for instance, were exhibited for all passers-by to see. Each picture was in a large frame, and in one corner was inserted a miniature photograph of her illustrious son. The portraits of many of those mothers were unfamiliar, but the message that was proclaimed was too great to miss. It is the mother who is great and the son who is small. The message spoken was clearly this: "She must increase but he must decrease." The mother is great even though she is obscure. And on the table in the midst of the portraits was a basket of apples and a Bible, as symbols of what a true home really is. There was also a motto in the window which everyone may well memorize: "Most of all the beautiful things in life come by twos or threes, by dozens and hundreds; plenty of roses, stars, sunsets, rainbows, brothers, sisters, aunts, cousins, but only one mother in the whole wide world."

In seeing this, one is reminded of Solomon, whose glory casts a spell over all history and of whom even our Lord spoke. After some centuries had passed, an immortal poet sang of King Solomon and of his mother in words that are memorable and unforgettable. This unknown poet spoke of "the crown wherewith his mother crowned him." That is worth thinking about. Every man is crowned with his mother's crown. Recently a well-known public man was introduced as a self-made man. Later he began to think about the question of being self-made. Was he self-made? Who gave him his fine physique? Whose blood flowed through his veins? Who gave him his sense of honor and integrity? When he thought about it and what he had inherited, he began to think of his mother and came to the conclusion that it was she who had placed whatever crown he wore upon his head.

It is said of Alexander the Great that he never wore any garments save those which were made by his mother's hands. There is a tradition, too, that the seamless garment that our Lord wore, which was stripped from him when he hung on the cross, had been woven for him by the gentle hands of his mother. These are symbols of an abiding fact. It is always a mother's hand that stitches into the garments her child wears the dreams and hopes of life. Many years ago when Grover Cleveland was sitting alone after his election as Governor of New York, he began to think of his early life, his apparent successes, and the future. He was writing a letter to his brother, and in it he said, "Do you know, if Mother were alive I would feel so much safer." There are men and women today who would feel safer if their mothers were alive. She would steady the hand and the heart and the step, and put inspiration and renewed ideals into the hearts of her grown sons and daughters.

Did you ever notice the way in which the Bible honors the mothers of men? They are placed in a hall of fame all their own. No matter whether he was a wise or a foolish, a righteous or an evil king, his mother's name is set down. It all runs something like this: His mother's name was Jochebed. His mother's name was Jehoaddan. His mother's name was Zibiah. His mother's name was Jecholiah. His mother's name was Jerusha. His mother's name was Abi. His mother's name was Hephzibah. His mother's name was Hamutal. His mother's name was Jedidah. His mother's name was Micaiah. His mother's name was Elizabeth. His mother's name was Mary. You will remember that it was a mother who said, "Grant that these my two sons may sit, the one on thy right hand, and the other on the left, in thy kingdom." It is always so. Who else but a mother has a right to demand that her children shall sit on thrones and be wreathed with crowns? It is also important for us to remember that Jesus did not deny the plea, but promised to grant the request if her children would prove worthy. Sometimes a mother's prayers fail, not because of what she has been or done, but because of the unworthiness of those who refuse the crown with which their mother would crown them.

There are two things that need to be said in this connection.

First of all, let us pause, every one, young and old, to pay tribute to the life and work of our mothers. Whether they are with us or have passed into the silence, it is well for us here and now to give them their true desert. It may not do them much good now, but it will do us good. It will steady us and humble us and put us in the way of faith and prayer and memory.

Herbert Spencer was one of the great minds of his generation. He had a great intellectual sweep that took in science and philosophy, education and logic, and history and religion. He wrought out in his day a comprehensive philosophy which took in the whole wide world, known and unknown. Toward the end of his life he wrote his autobiography. There we find him speaking of his mother, and this is what he says: "She was a woman of ordinary intelligence and of high moral nature. She was never sufficiently prized. Speaking broadly, the world is divided into two classes: those who deserve little and get much, and those who deserve much and get little; and it is a source of unceasing regret to me that my mother belonged to the latter class."

Let us see to it that we do not give voice to such regrets. Let us see to it that the one who has done so much to put our feet in the path of life is sufficiently prized. However we give our gratitude, let it be in a way that she will understand. One of the touching things in the story of Jesus is his remembrance of his mother on the dark day of his crucifixion. He was not too much occupied with his own agony and his own dying to think of his mother.

In the second place, let us think of the opportunity that every mother has. It is a strange world into which our children are born. It is a world that has gone far from the standards of our mother's day. There are some things that are better. There are improvements in some things. But the world into which children come today is a dangerous world, so difficult that one wonders at the courage of parents in entrusting their children to the currents of life that move so swiftly. The time into which children come is an important era in history and the destiny of our nation, as has often been said, is in the hands of the mothers who are training the children of today.

The president of a university was heard telling a story about a principal of a school who had made a success out of a boy who had been incorrigible. When school was dismissed, the bad boy found himself seated at the principal's desk copying out on a white sheet of paper all the offenses he had committed during the year. When he had written for five minutes, he showed the paper to the principal, who, in turn, opened a drawer in the desk and took out a record book. Turning to the bad boy's name, he began to read the record he had kept of every offense for which the boy had been punished. Again the boy set to work to make the record of his bad deeds complete. After several reminders, the boy finished his list of bad deeds. Then he was given a fresh sheet of paper and told to write a sentence about each of his offenses, explaining why he had done them. When this was done, he was told to copy all that he had written on another clean, white paper. By this time the darkness was coming down and the boy was feeling weary and hungry. "Now," said the principal, "take this sheet and with pen and ink make as good a copy as you can and we will send it home to your mother." "Oh, no!" said the boy, and tears came to his eyes. "Why not?" asked the principal. "Because I don't want my mother to know about this." "But doesn't your mother know what sort of boy you are?" the principal asked. "No, she doesn't," said the boy. "Does she think you are a good boy?" the principal asked. And through his stammering words, the boy answered, "Yes." "And so," the principal went on, "you don't want your mother to know what sort of boy you are at school. But I don't see how we can help it, for I've tried everything I know to do. Let me think a minute." The principal walked up and down the room, as the boy tried to dry away the tears he was ashamed of. Finally he said, "Do you think you could be the sort of boy your mother thinks you are?" The boy thought he could. "Well, then, I'll tell you what we'll do. We will put what you have written in this large envelope and seal it and put it away in my safe. If you are not sent up to me again, we will just put the whole thing in the furnace and say no more about it." And his mother never knew, except this: that he became the kind of boy she thought he was.

Let no mother despair of her work or her prayers. The great bishop of Milan Ambrose said to Monica, the mother of a wayward, prodigal son: " Go thy way. It is not possible for the prayers of such a mother to go unanswered." They were not unanswered, and that wayward son became an important leader of the Church, known as Saint Augustine. It is not possible for the prayers of a mother to go unanswered, for when all the years are gone, she will discover her children wearing the crowns wherewith she crowned them.

8

What Has War Taught Us?

[A MEMORIAL DAY SERMON]

" *Then Samuel took a stone, and set it between Mizpeh and Shen, and called the name of it Ebenezer, saying, Hitherto hath the Lord helped us.*" — I Sam. 7:12.

THE Philistines had surrendered unconditionally to their age-old enemy. The battle had been conclusive and Samuel, who was prophet, priest, and king, in order to commemorate the victory, took a stone and set it up on the battlefield and called it " Ebenezer." The word " Ebenezer " is now a good English word and has found its way into the hymnal and into the dictionary. It means " the stone of help," and its interpretation is to the effect that " Hitherto hath the Lord helped us." It was a memorial stone, a stone of remembrance, a stone of thanksgiving. On this Memorial Day we too should think of erecting our Ebenezer, our memorial to the goodness of God and the brave men who have fallen in battle.

It is interesting to notice that no man's name was engraved upon that historic stone of Old Testament fame. Probably in those days of old they had their Eisenhowers and their MacArthurs too, but no name of any soldier or leader was engraved there. It was what we would call a " Te Deum," bearing the message, " We praise thee, O God; we acknowledge thee to be the

Lord." And as we look back over the dreadful nights of conflict, it is to God that we lift our hearts in gratitude and hope. How vivid our memories are, which, through the continuance of war's menace, have not been allowed even yet to die! The guns, once silent, still roar; the airplanes, once grounded, fly again; the ships, once called home, sail the seas in angry pursuit. War, with all its tragedy and sorrow, still demands its prize and we ask ourselves the questions: "What have we learned from these dark days? What has war taught us? What memorial have we to give? What stone of remembrance can we erect?"

First of all, we surely have learned something about the tragic and terrible abyss humanity can make for itself. War has taught us what we did not believe, how bad man can be. We had come to believe that progress was inevitable, that evolution was the first law of life, and that all men needed was money and food and freedom in order to rise upon steppingstones to their highest ideal. We had thought that all men needed was a chance to have a job, to have a good home, to pursue the good neighbor policy, to treat every man as a born brother, and then we should regain our paradise. It was a common thought in the minds of men that sin was outmoded or reserved merely for the pulpit, and that the modern man and woman need not worry about their own sins or the sin of the world. It would be a good world, with all modern inventions, and leisure would be the rule of life rather than work. So we believed.

And then all of a sudden we saw humanity fall from heaven like Lucifer. All of a sudden we saw and heard so many unspeakable things that were too horrible to believe. So unbelieving, so unspeakable, so terrible were these things that certain persons after war's end were commissioned to go and see with their own eyes what war had done. Death chambers, torture camps, human incinerators, warehouses crammed with the belongings of countless dead, shoes and garments of innocent children. This is what war had done. War had taught us how to hate. War taught us the futility of life. War gave new meaning to the word "annihilism." War made our blood boil. But that should not be the deepest result of such a record. We should be led down the path of humility and penitence that such a revelation of human nature is possible. It is this fact of fallen humanity that creates the problem of the world for our day. It is easy indeed to put war criminals to death, but what can we do with the people who have been trained and taught to think and act as beasts? What a revelation of the possibilities of human nature war has been, calling upon us to return in strength to the proclamation of the gospel that what man needs is not merely reformation but redemption, and what the world needs is a religious awakening that will change the moral standards of mankind.

In contradiction to all this, we must say, in the second place, that we have learned to understand something of the amazing heights to which men and women can attain. War has revealed heroism displayed all along the line of battle by those whose names have been headlined and by those whose names will never appear in print. We think of that strong band of Christian people who resisted the downward drive of evil spirits, believing that heaven and earth could pass away but the Word of God could not pass away. We think of man like the chaplain on the battered and broken *U.S.S. Franklin* who fought through fire and flame and who later said, "I don't mind being blown up with the ship; for those who believe in God death is a transition between earth and heaven." We think of other outstanding Christian heroes, but we think also of the young men and women whose names are known only to their families and to the records, who have gone forth inspired by high and noble ideals to do what in their hearts they did not want to do. They rose above everything selfish and endured, seeing the invisible, and everywhere they bore themselves with courage, patience, and faith. A visitor to a veterans' hospital tried to sympathize with a soldier who had lost his leg, saying, "I am sorry you lost your leg." The lad replied: "I didn't lose it. I bought a clean conscience with it." Let us take time to think through that remark, for it represents the thinking of the vast army of youth that has won for us the right to be free.

In the third place, war has revealed to us the sureness of God's judgment. How slow the judgment of God seems to be, how uncertain it seems! At the same time it is difficult for us who have been trained in the Christian faith to keep our demand for judgment and justice burning bright. It is easy to become softhearted and forgiving and generous. We forget the crimes and the guilt too easily. We are placed in the paradoxical position between justice and mercy and we will remember that vengeance does not belong to us. It is as if Jesus came in our midst, weeping in agony over the cities of destruction and saying, " O . . . thou that killest the prophets, and stonest them which are sent unto thee, how often would I have gathered thy children together, even as a hen gathereth her chickens under her wings, and ye would not! "

What are we to do in the face of justice? After the archcriminals have been dealt with, and the high command has been dealt with, and the financiers and industrialists have been dealt with, what are we going to do with the people who permit such things to take place? What will we do with those who plan war and seek war and make war an instrument of policy? What shall we say to those who already think of another day when other wars will devastate the earth? What kind of world would it be if it were to fall permanently into the hands of such people? But now judgment is knocking at the door. There is something in the very constitution of the universe, something wrought in the very warp and woof of the world, that reveals that at the heart of history there is some moral principle at work. Perhaps sometime, somehow, the world will return to penitence and to prayer and to trust in Almighty God. It not only will be so but it must be so, for only as we see the truth in God do we find our way to peace and happiness and good will.

It is good for us to have this day when we can look below the surface and see that we have passed through a time of real consecration. It is a time for silence and prayer and thoughtfulness, when the spirit of vengeance is absent and the desire for justice universally present. It is a time to remember that we are Christians and to believe that God is on his throne and that a rainbow of mercy arches his sovereignty.

Kaj Munk was a Danish martyr of the Second World War. He was a patriot, preacher, and poet. Preaching his last sermon in the Cathedral of Copenhagen, he was found next day dead in a ditch. In his sermon, just before he was murdered, he said: "To remain silent when face to face with evil is to speak the language of the devil. When the war has reached its sanguinary end, the Prince of Darkness will cry aloud from all the graves of vengeance. We too know some with whom there are scores to settle. But this must be done in the name of God and not of the devil. Let us be sure of that."

We too have some scores to settle but let us also be sure that the settlement be made in the name of God and not of the devil. What is done in victory let it be done in the name of God, remembering the ancient words: "The Lord God is long-suffering, and of great mercy, forgiving iniquity and transgression, and by no means clearing the guilty, visiting the iniquity of the fathers upon the children unto the third and the fourth generation." He is the judge and he will do what is right in his own eyes. "When the Son of man shall come in his glory, . . . then shall he sit upon the throne of his glory: and before him" — *before him* — "shall be gathered all nations: and he shall separate them one from another." Let this then be our Ebenezer. Let this be our stone of rememberance. Let this be our prayer. "Into thy hand, O God, we commit ourselves and all men."

9

A Day for Hope

[AN INDEPENDENCE DAY SERMON]

"*Why art thou cast down, O my soul?*
And why art thou disquieted in me?
Hope thou in God: for I shall yet praise him
For the help of his countenance." — Ps. 42:5.

THE Fourth of July has always been a day of hope and opportunity. As our minds run back over the pages of time, history seems to say, "Lift up your hearts." And again and again the response has come, "We lift them up unto the Lord."

A religion that does not inspire hope is a religion not worth bothering about. A religion that discourages and burdens and throws a cloud over the face of the future is not a religion that can be called a gospel. The Christian religion is a religion of hope. It is a singing religion. It is a religion of the morning, of the springtime, of the sunshine. It sounds the note of the trumpet.

The apostle Paul described the world of his day as a world without hope. The people to whom the message of the evangel came are described as being without hope, without God, adrift in a godless world. In the life of Nansen, the Norwegian explorer, in a day when there was no radio, it is said that after he had been absent for thirty months, in his search for the North Pole, one day a carrier pigeon came to the window of his home in Norway bearing the message out of the frozen North that "all is well." It had come over a thousand miles of ice and snow, a white-winged messenger of hope. The gospel is a white-winged messenger of hope.

When Christianity came to our pagan ancestors, it came to them as a message of hope. Paulinus, the eloquent missionary, presented the gospel to King Edwin of England. The king called a council of his wise men, and they met near the village of York in the year 627. The chief priest of paganism cynically said that the pagan gods had done nothing for them, and that he was ready to try another religion. Then one of the nobles said: "O King, often at a feast in the hall in winter when the warm fire is lighted and the cold storm is without, a sparrow is seen entering the warm room and then flying out into the winter darkness. So it is with us. What has gone before, what comes after, no man can tell; but if the stranger can give us any hope as to the things to come, let him be heard."

Then Paulinus, the herald of the evangel, spoke. He told the old, old story and when he had finished, the king said: "Now I understand what the truth is. I see it shining clearly in the message of hope." The bringing in of a better hope brought in the day of a better life. The old pagan temple was destroyed, and in its place a little Christian church was built; and on the spot there stands today the York Minster, one of the great cathedrals of

Christendom, testifying to the living hope born of the gospel.

It is not to be wondered at that, with the revival of secularism in our land, our age is face to face with a rebirth of hopelessness. A sense of despair has fallen upon Western civilization. The note of defeat is being sounded in government, in education, in family life, and even in religion. General MacArthur was near the truth when he suggested that the policy of America toward world order is being dictated by fear. As crime becomes common, we have grown increasingly callous, while men mock at law and truth. We must lay the blame where it belongs. When men laugh in the face of God and make light of his word and his will, can we expect other than a famine of hope and faith? Let America return to God, to reverence for his ways; and the depression and despair which have fallen upon us will vanish like clouds before the sun. Hope is born of faith in God, and a God who is holy, just, and true is the pledge that the dreams and hopes of all the years will find a blessed fulfillment.

Of all the books in the world the Bible is the most hopeful because it enthrones God. From the rainbow promise in Genesis to the " river of water of life, clear as crystal " in Revelation the pages of the Bible abound in hope. Much of modern literature is full of gloom. The Bible is a book that excels in gladness. Our literature ends in defeat and darkness. The Bible is a book that ends in triumph and delight. It is filled with poetry that sings and shouts. The stories of this Book end in wedding festivals and songs of victory. Joseph is rescued from the pit and is made a prime minister. Ruth, the alien, comes out of proverty and distress into a rich and happy inheritance. Job is revived from his despair and set once more among his children and friends. Greatest of all, Jesus died on the cross only on the third day to rise from the dead as the Easter morning began to break.

It is no wonder that Christianity is a religion of hope. Jesus is the most hopeful life known to men. When he came, the angels sang. When he departed, a multitude that no man could number lifted up their voices in praise. This is nothing sentimental or superficial. No one entered more deeply into the heart of life's tragedies than did Jesus. No one ever understood human nature as Jesus understood it. The modern psychologist, with his revelation of the dark things that move in the jungle of a man's underworld, does not speak such sharp, stinging words as did Jesus concerning the depravity and subtlety that characterize humanity. All the deception and duplicity, the hypocrisy and fraud, that man is capable of and holds up to scorn in a modern newspaper, was understood and analyzed by Jesus. "Out of the heart," he said, "proceed evil thoughts, murders, adulteries, fornifications, thefts, false witness, blasphemies: These are the things which defile a man." Knowing all this, Jesus nevertheless had a sublime hopefulness concerning human nature. He never lost hope in men and women. He lifted them up by his high hopefulness, because he knew them to be children of God.

The New Testament speaks of a "living hope [A.S.V.]." "According to his abundant mercy, God hath begotten us again unto a living hope." That is a fine phrase. We know what a dead hope is, but this is a living hope. Probably the greatest symbol of hope that our modern world knows is embodied in the painting by the Christian artist George Frederic Watts. It is the picture of a girl, blindfolded, sitting on an empty world, with a broken harp in her hand and playing upon a single remaining string. This is a beautiful and spiritual interpretation of hope. It is possible to make music even on a broken lyre with a single string. It is possible to sing even when blindfolded and not being able to see or understand. One would, however, hardly call that a "living hope." The New Testament speaks of hope as a triumphant virtue which causes the heart of man to cry out: "Hope thou in God; for I shall yet praise him, who is the help of my countenance, and my God [A.S.V.]."

Men of God in all ages have carried on in the spirit of a "living hope." It is said that hope burned like a living fire in the life of Oliver Cromwell. On this Independence Day we think of the hope that sustained the founders of this nation, which enabled them to see the sun rising out of the thick clouds. Carlyle tells us that when John Knox came to the end of his hard and strenuous life hope won its greatest victory. He had had defeats and misfortunes. He had been a galley slave and a wanderer in exile. Before the end came, the comrades around his bed asked him, "Have you hope?" "Have you hope?" they asked him, when he could no longer speak. He lifted his hand and with his finger pointed upward and so died, sustained by a "living hope."

So, on this important occasion, may this be our prayer:

> "In hope that sends a shining ray
> Far down the future's broadening way;
> In peace that only Thou canst give,
> With Thee, O Master, let me live."

10

The Sin of Thanklessness

[A THANKSGIVING DAY SERMON]

"*Because that, when they knew God, they glorified him not as God, neither were thankful; but became vain in their imaginations, and their foolish heart was darkened.*" — Rom. 1:21.

THANKSGIVING DAY is a time when we express our thanks to Almighty God for our national and personal blessings. Thankfulness is the mark of a good life. Thanklessness is the mark of an unfinished life. Thanklessness is classed among the vices. In the first chapter of Romans, as you read through the passage, you find that thanklessness is listed with immorality and other crimes.

The first chapter of Paul's Letter to the Romans is so spotted with dark and damning sins that it can scarcely be read in public. Like the knife of a surgeon, Paul's pen opens up a festering mess of pagan immorality. Let us sum up his findings: wickedness, covetousness, malice, envy, murder, strife, deceit, malignity, gossip, slander, sensuality, hatred, insolence, boastfulness, disobedience, foolishness, faithlessness, heartlessness, ruthlessness. And at the last: thanklessness. Taking rank among all these base and deadly sins is thanklessness. Was it not said,

> "How sharper than a serpent's tooth it is
> To have a thankless child!"?

A thankless person is all wrapped up in himself and, as has been said, a person all wrapped up in himself makes a very small parcel. He is like the old medieval palace — luxurious, palatial, inviting. Gradually the walls crowd in, the ceiling lowers, the floor rises, and it contracts into a prison house. It is self-destroying. Our medical friends warn us of the germs of disease. They are invisible, invading life everywhere, destroying and devastating. And yet, I have read somewhere that perhaps there are germs of health that pass from blood stream to blood stream, spreading healthy-mindedness, good cheer, and thankfulness, passing on something of an invisible vitality. I am sure that must be true. I have known just such people. To be with them is like drinking the elixir of life.

Take this same Paul, whose words blast and burn. See how he can express his thankfulness: "I thank my God always on your behalf"; "I thank my God upon every remembrance of you"; "I thank my God . . . for you all." Let us take time to count over the names of those for whom we have cause to be grateful. Let us thread their names as beads on a rosary of gratitude — all those who have helped us and been to us like music in a dark land. What blessings are there that bring memories of gratitude?

There is *life*. It is God's gift to us. If God gave us this greater gift, will he not give us the lesser gifts? What simple things they are of which Jesus speaks — bread, drink, clothing! How little we really need and yet how much we want! It is America with its high standard of living, not Africa in its poverty, that frets itself about what it does not have. Thank God for life.

Thank God for *what you have*. Jesus said that the heathen worry about what they do not have. Christians thank God for what they have. Heathen people are always seeking, always dissatisfied. Christians know how to be content. They know, as Paul said, "how to be abased and, . . . how to abound." Count your blessings. You will be surprised. Did you ever walk with a little child in the night and try to count the stars — one, two, ten, forty, ninety — until he grew tired and said, "I never knew how many there are"? Thank God for what you have.

Thank God for *the world*. Turn your thought away from yourself. Watch the world as it goes on around you. Follow the advice of the psalmist, who said, "I will lift up mine eyes unto the hills." The outside world will give us perspective, and we shall learn that seedtime and harvest, summer and winter, day and night will not fail us. "Consider the lilies," said Jesus, and see "how they grow." Thank God for America. Consider its rivers and forests and valleys and plains. I have seen pictures of other lands, but I know there is something in America that makes me sing,

"O beautiful for spacious skies,
For amber waves of grain,
For purple mountain majesties
Above the fruited plain!"

What bountiful harvests we have which have fed ourselves and other people. And yet what a complaining people we are! What progress we have made! And yet we are not satisfied. How much there is to give us comfort and good living! But we are restless.

Thank God for *today*. Tomorrow will take care of itself. "Sufficient unto the day is the evil therof," were Jesus' words. Take each day, with its care and its opportunity, as it comes. Think of Cardinal Newman's prayer as your prayer: "I do not ask to see the distant scene — one step enough for me." Thank God for what you can do and do not worry about what you cannot do. Certainly this is a hard world. Jesus never promised that it would be an easy world. That is why he called upon the people to follow him. "In me," he said, "ye shall have peace." One of God's servants who knew something about this world's trouble has given us a way to follow:

"If thou but suffer God to guide thee,
And hope in Him thro' all thy ways,
He'll give thee strength, whate'er betide thee,
And bear thee thro' the evil days;
Who trusts in God's unchanging love
Builds on the rock that naught can move."

What we need is to awaken gratitude. During the dark days in Great Britain when the food lines were lengthening, Sir Stafford Cripps, speaking for the Treasury, said: " I wish that today our country could express its heart and mind with a deep draught of that Christian faith which has come down to us over two thousand years and has over those centuries inspired the peoples of Europe to fresh efforts and new hopes. It is that spirit and not our own material hopes and difficulties that can be the most potent source of our inspiration. Call it by what name you will — self-sacrifice, honor, love, comradeship — it is the strongest power in our lives and at this moment of deep difficulty in our history, we need its supporting strength as never before." We all say " Amen " to that. Let us lay hold of the invisible. Let us lift up our hearts and be thankful. Let us thank God for our Christian faith.

A journalist of distinction was reporting on the sickening conditions in war-ravaged countries. He was reporting to an elder statesman. Both men were sick at heart. The elder statesman rose from his seat and lifted a bowl of blood-red roses from the table. " Do you like roses? " he said. " Like them? " was the reply. " I love them." " Then bury your face in this loveliness and thank God." With all the dark lines in the sky, with all the dark words in our reading, with all the discouragements and disillusionments about us, let us bury ourselves in the transfiguring loveliness of God as he is revealed in the gospel and then let us set forth to face the future in good cheer, remembering, as we go, the assurance of Jesus: " In the world ye shall have tribulation: but be of good cheer; I have overcome the world."

Section Three

THE CHRISTIAN FAITH

11

The Christian Way to Think About God

"*God is a Spirit: and they that worship him must worship him in spirit and in truth.*" — John 4:24.

THE deepest need of the world is a fresh vision of God. Every new era in the world's history has been ushered in by the deepening of the religious convictions of mankind. Every religious awakening has depended upon a new insight into the character of God. A man's thought of God determines the value of his religion and the quality of his life. If we know how a man thinks about God, we know the nature of his religious temper and the measure of his character. As the moon draws the water of the ocean in the great sweep of the tidal wave, so does man's thought of God determine destiny and make history.

A scholarly layman has said that the average man's idea of God is too vague to be communicable. Doubtless this is true, for there is no more indefinite and colorless word in our language than the word "God." It is used by the people of all religions. The Hindu uses it and reads into it his indiscriminate pantheism. The Moslem uses it with all its contradictory associations. The Buddhist and the Christian use it, but part company concerning its appropriate meaning. Chinese pilgrims climb the sacred slopes of Tai Shan and discover at the summit the "Inscriptionless Monument," a block of granite fifteen feet high and four feet wide. Centuries before the Christian Era, it was carried there and became to pious patriots the symbol of the mystery of life. No word was graven on its surface but centuries ago someone carved at its base the Chinese character for God. It was an attempt to give an answer. That is as far as China could go. But it leaves us with a colorless name. It does not bring us into the presence of One to whom we can say: "Our Father which art in heaven, Hallowed be thy name. Thy kingdom come. Thy will be done." Apart from Christ this is as far as the world can go.

In *The Forsyte Saga,* John Galsworthy tells of the conversation of a father and his son as they stood together beside the grave of a little dog which they had both dearly loved. Speaking as if to himself, the father said, "Strange life, a dog's, the only four-footer with the rudiments of altruism, and a sense of God." Jolly looked at his father. "Do you believe in God, Dad? I've never known." At so searching a question from one to whom it was impossible to make a light reply, Jolyon stood for a moment. "What do you mean by God?" he said. "There are two irreconciliable ideas of God. There's the Unknowable Creative Principle — one believes in that. And there's the Sum of Altruism in man — naturally one believes in that." "I see," said the boy, "that leaves out Christ, doesn't it?"

We shall never get far in our thought of God if we leave Christ out. We must begin with him and when we begin with him, we begin with God. Jesus began with God. He took God for granted. He did not argue about him. We seek to prove him. Jesus revealed him. The first volume of Charles Hodge's *Theology* has four hundred pages of discussion devoted to proofs for the existence of God. The *Encyclopædia Britannica* has thirteen closely printed pages, double columns, devoted to the arguments for the existence of God. Jesus took all that for granted. He never sought to convert men to believing in God. He knew that no man is an atheist at heart. Even Voltaire said if there were no God, it would be necessary to invent one. That is what the philosophers of Athens attempted to do when they erected an altar with the inscription "TO THE UNKNOWN GOD." Jesus "knew what was in man." He knew that as the hart pants after the water brooks, so the heart of humanity longs after God. This is an age-old argument and its force is still undiminished.

Jesus came not to prove God but to make God known. He came to reveal the nature and character of God. What is that revelation, we ask? The New Testament sums it up in three very short sentences which are as spiritual as they are simple, far removed from any crude symbolism, describing God in terms of human thought and life. Only in such terms can we understand God. "Nothing can be good in Him which evil is in me." These are the three sentences: "God is a Spirit"; "God is light"; "God is love."

First, "God is a Spirit." Jesus swept away the misconceptions of his age regarding a national God, but he clarified the thought of his time concerning the nature of God. God is a spirit. What is a spirit? We may not be able to tell what a spirit is, but we can tell what a spirit does. A spirit thinks and feels and wills. A spirit is self-conscious. A spirit knows, understands, perceives, and directs itself. In other words, a spirit is a person. We are spirits and God, who is the Father of our spirits, cannot be less personal than we are. He must be the only real person in the world. I am not yet a true person. My will is not in harmony with my thinking. I pursue a sort of double existence. My thought wars against my will. My will antagonizes and defies my best feelings.

In God, however, willing, feeling, and knowing exist in happy harmony and perfect unity. He, then, is the only perfect person. He alone perfectly thinks and feels and wills. He is free. He is in all and over all. He is self-conscious, self-directing. He is not a prisoner in his own universe, as the life of a tree is imprisoned in root and trunk and branch. God is inexhaustible in his life, transcendent in his energy. If we mean by personality something inseparable from the physical, the human, the limited, we are not thinking in terms of the New Testament. When we say that God is a Person, when we say that God is a Spirit, we mean that he is conscious of himself, self-directing, the Father of our spirits. Before such a God we worship and adore. In his presence we find reality in worship and reasonableness in prayer. We are created in his image, in his likeness; he is our Father, the Father of our spirits. Because we are such, we answer to the challenge, "Speak to Him, thou, for He hears, and Spirit with Spirit can meet." This is the basis for prayer, for fellowship, for communion with God.

Secondly, "God is light." The Christian revelation contains the further word that God is as good as the light, as winsome, as crystal-pure, as incorruptible, as sincere as the sunlight, uncontaminated, sweet and full of wholesome healing, driving away the darkness of doubt and fear, bringing in hope and health and happiness. When Christ came the people who walked in darkness saw a great light. God became to men the Father of lights in whom is no shadow, no suggestion of evil, the central sun of all life. In the City of God there is need for neither sun nor stars, for the Lord God himself gives the light, and the glory of God lightens it. Because he is the center of the moral universe, we know that day will not die down in darkness. It gives us confidence to know that. We need to know that in God men find fellowship, because light is social. It is darkness that separates. It is light and purity and unity that create fellowship and link us with all that is good and great.

The poet Browning speaks of Judas wandering alone on the very edge of the universe "made monstrous through much solitude." It is sin and evil that segregate men and nations. If we do not walk in the light, then it becomes a destroying agency rather than a beneficial messenger. A child may take a piece of glass and with it resist the streams of light that come in healing ministry over millions of miles, and bring forth fire and flame. Nations that resist the light which is meant to heal and bless will find themselves shriveled in its flame. It is part of the revelation that "our God is a consuming fire."

Thirdly, "God is love." From the world with its sun and moon and stars, with its forces and its mysteries, Jesus leads out into a home, and lets us see a family with father, mother, and little children. God, said Jesus, is even more than father and mother.

What do we mean by "God is love"? We use the phrase in a glib and superficial way, as if it were easy to believe in a God of love in a world like this. How can we find it easy to believe that God cares, in view of the facts of life which all of us must sooner or later face? Is it easy to believe that God is love during the tragedy of war or at a time of sudden and unexpected death? Even on the cross our Lord said, "My God, . . . why . . . ?"

It is all very well to speak superficially of finding love at the heart of the universe, but for many it is the most difficult of all Christian doctrines. What is love? Apart from Saint Paul's great revelation, one of the best definitions of love is given by Tolstoy, who said, "When you love a person, you do for that person what that person needs." It is a low, unworthy love that seeks merely to obtain, to get, to possess. Love is true to itself when it reaches beyond the selfish and seeks to share and sacrifice. Love does for others that which they need. They may need sympathy or they may need sternness. Love does not shrink from any task. It never fails. It is seen in the patriot who gives his life for his country. It is seen in the scientist who gives his all for truth. It is seen in the mother who gives and withholds nothing. We cannot expect less of God than we do of a mother. That is why there is something of a moral obligation about the cross. There is a compulsion, a necessity about Calvary; for God, since God is love, must do for his own all that they need.

Do we understand what this means? Jesus understood it and said to his bewildered and doubting followers, "Ought not the Christ to have suffered these things, and to enter into his glory?" He must do for his own all that they need. He must go all the way from Bethlehem to Calvary. There and there only do we understand that, even in a world of pain, God is love. At Calvary, God "commendeth his love toward us." This is the Christian way to think about God. God was in Christ. If we surrender the revelation of God in Christ, we are no farther on our way than Plato or Socrates or Aristotle. If we accept the truth that in the life and death and resurrection of Christ God was incarnate, we have entered into the final truth concerning Him who is Father of our spirits, the Light of our lives, the Saviour of our souls.

12

The Christian Way to Think About Jesus Christ

"And Simon Peter answered and said, Thou art the Christ, the Son of the living God." — Matt. 16:16.

DOWN through the ages the question has been asked, "Who is Jesus Christ?" Many answers have been given. He has been called, "The first true gentleman that ever lived." Will that answer suffice? "O man's best Man, O love's best Love." Will that do? "The highest, holiest manhood Thou." Will that do? "One Lord Jesus Christ, the only-begotten Son of God, begotten of His Father before all worlds; God of God; Light of Light; Very God of Very God; Begotten, not made; . . . Who for us men, and for our salvation, came down from heaven." Will that do? If it does suffice, how can we bridge the chasm that separates us from him?

It is a highly important fact to observe that Jesus himself asked this same question. After he had been with his disciples two years, he took them apart for a quiet time into a region of unforgettable beauty and there, alone with them, he asked this question: "Whom do men say that I, the Son of man, am?" It is a strange question for anyone to ask. It suggests oddness and mystery. He wanted to know what the people in the towns and villages thought of him. "Whom do men say that I am?" And they answered him: "Some say that thou art John the Baptist, some, Elias; and others, Jeremias, or one of the prophets" — perhaps Amos, or Hosea, or Daniel. That is, they put him among their great men, their heroes. They did what is sometimes done today: they put him among the six or ten greatest men of all time. That is what is often done and men say that Jesus was a genius, a superman. And that is good as far as it goes, but it only touches the hem of his garment.

If you remember the story, Jesus was not satisfied with this answer and so he pressed his question. "Yes, that is what the people say, but you, you who have been with me day and night and heard my words and seen my deeds, what do you say; who do *you* say that I am?" And Peter, speaking for his comrades, said, "Thou art the Christ, the Son of the living God." I do not know all that Peter meant by these mysterious words. My library is full of explanations and interpretations of them. They are still an undiscovered vocabulary. Perhaps Peter himself did not fully know, for he did not long sustain his confession, and Jesus says it came as a heavenly revelation. It was like a flash of inspiration. It was like an inner revealing, like insight that is flashed from some unknown lighthouse of the Spirit. But Jesus knew and understood and was satisfied. "Blessed art thou, Simon Bar-jona: for flesh and blood hath not revealed it unto thee, but my Father which is in heaven."

Blessing follows that discovery. It does make a difference what our doctrine of Jesus is. If Jesus is only one of the prophets, then we will garnish his sepulcher and make pilgrimages to his shrine.

> "If Jesus Christ is a God—
> And the only God, —I swear
> I will follow him through heaven and hell,
> The earth, the sea, and the air."
> —*From "The Song of a Heathen," by Richard W. Gilder.*

Peter's confession satisfied Jesus and it satisfies us. The conviction that he is the Son of the living God captured the world. It drove every idol from its throne. It condemned and judged society. It conquered the conscience of the world, and before we can conquer the conscience of our complex modern world, we too must be mastered by this conviction. It is not the conviction of a theological theory, but the conviction of a living faith; a passion that stakes its fears, its gifts, its hopes, upon the fact of the living Christ.

John is dead. Elijah is dead. Jeremiah is dead. All the prophets are dead and are powerless, save as they live in lives made better by their presence; but Christ is alive. Dr. Denny, the distinguished theologian, has pointed out that no New Testament writer ever went back into the past "to remember Christ." By this he meant that Christ was not thought of as belonging to the past. He is not merely the Christ of history. He is the Christ of experience. He is our contemporary. The disciples thought of him as living with them and guiding them. He is the Son of the living God. This truth is brought out in the message that Festus sent to Agrippa, in which he charged Paul with preaching and proclaiming " one Jesus, which was dead, whom Paul affirmed to be alive." That was the secret of the Christian's power. The living Christ is not confined to any age or to any locality. He is alive forevermore. That experience transformed the world, and it is that experience which again can transform the world. It is the gospel of the living God, the glad tidings of the living Christ, " the same yesterday, today, and forever." He cannot be enshrined in any creed or embodied in any history or analyzed by any metaphysics, but lives in the lives of those who love him, and he is with his disciples in every country and in every age.

Sir Philip Gibbs, the eminent correspondent of the First World War, in summing up the conclusions to which he had come, out of deep experience and long thought, pictures a future which is not promising. He contends that there is disease and insanity in our present social order, and wonders if the world can be cured of its cruelty and stupidity. Nevertheless, he says, " My own belief is that the war was no proof against the Christian faith, but rather a revelation that we are as desperately in need of the Spirit of Christ as at any time in the history of mankind." This is the message our halting, hesitating, halfhearted world needs. We are desperately in need of Christ. He alone is our hope. He alone can cure our social order of its stupidity, and guarantee the human heart peace. He alone is the Rock of Ages, the chief cornerstone in the temple of redeemed humanity.

When Shackleton came to the end of his long, perilous trip across South Georgia Island, a perilous march of thirty-six hours over mountains of ice, he looked into the faces of his two companions, and said, " It seemed to me often that we were four, not three." They had a strange feeling on that dangerous march that an unseen Comrade was with them. That is the experience of the living presence of the Eternal Christ. Shackleton found that companionship in the ice fields of the South Antarctic, and the three tried and persecuted young men of The Book of Daniel found that same presence in the midst of the furnace of fire. "Lo, I see four men loose, walking in the midst of fire, and they have no hurt; and the form of the fourth is like the Son of God."

It was upon this faith that the Christian Church was built. This faith is simple, so simple that a child may understand it. It is also dark with mystery, so that the philosopher and the sage may not fully comprehend. It has deep significance. We believe in the Christ of history. We believe that he "was conceived by the Holy Ghost, born of the Virgin Mary, suffered under Pontius Pilate, was crucified, dead, and buried; He descended into hell; the third day He rose again from the dead." That is history, but it is a step forward in faith to be able to say, "I know whom I have believed." The experience of the living Christ brings us into possession of a knowledge that nothing in earth can shake. It is no use for you or for me to have a philosophy about Christ, to classify him with the prophets or with the sages of the past, if we do not know him as our everliving Lord. Sometime you will have to come to terms with Jesus Christ. Why not now?

13

The Christian Way to Think About Man

"But one in a certain place testified, saying,
What is man, that thou art mindful of him?
Or the son of man, that thou visitest him?"
— Heb. 2:6.

THE question that is thrusting itself into our bewildered world is the age-old question, "What is man?" Behind all the political philosophies that are competing for our vote, this question intrudes. When we have found political and economic security, if we ever do, it will be because we have found an answer to this fundamental question. Behind the searching criticism that pervades modern literature and perplexes social scientists, this primary issue is constantly demanding consideration.

On the whole, two answers are given. The answers are as old as man himself. They can be found in the Bible. They can be found in modern life. To the question, "What is man?" the answer is given that man is a machine, a very delicate and useful machine but a machine that in turn will wear out and be thrown on the scrap heap. This is the teaching of Marxian Communism. Man is useful to the state, but he has no intrinsic value. On the other hand, the answer is given that man is a person, made in the image of God, with inalienable rights, destined to endure beyond the reach of time and the shock of death.

It may be difficult in our world to hold to this high and spiritual conception of man. The Bible senses this difficulty. It speaks of man as an enigma. Man is made a little lower than the angels, a little lower than God, he is crowned with glory and honor; but as we see him, the crown has been taken from his head and he is a slave. Instead of being master of the world, there is much that masters him, and, by a strange turn of logic, it is said that while we see man subordinate, yet we see one Man — Jesus; and he is crowned with glory and honor. Let us examine this thesis.

How little man seems when compared with our boundless universe, as it is seen through the 200-inch telescope! The ancients even in their day looked into the clear, starry sky and exclaimed, "When I consider thy heavens, the work of thy fingers, the moon and the stars, . . . What is man?" But today we know that each star we see is a sun and that there are accompanying it millions of stars we cannot see. You know that one of these stars could accommodate within itself some 60,000,000 of our suns and still have room for more. In such a universe, what is man? His life is a weaver's thread that is cut before the pattern is perfected; a dream, a sleep, a tale that is told, a vapor that appears for a little while, a shadow cast by the passing sunlight, a flower of the field beautiful in the morning but dying at the close of day, grass that grows up and withers, water spilled upon the ground.

Furthermore, when we look around we are not greatly encouraged by what we see. We have seen man broken, carrying about with him a sense of failure. We become indignant at the revelations of cruelty, indignity, and inhumanity. The newspapers puzzle and disillusion us, but the reality is worse than the revelation. The failure, the fall of man, is a tragic experience for every one of us. We are not the men or women we would like to be, and the deep gulf fixed between the real and the ideal is the revelation of our downfall. You can go to the East and you can see the splendor of ancient civilizations in the grandeur of the ruins that remain to surprise you, and you can see the same in the world of men. No one of us but has lived long enough to see the wrecks of humanity thrown upon the highways of life, broken pillars in the temple that is being made without hands, men and women who have been shorn of their influence and their right to power.

What is man? Can we find anywhere a true specimen? Must we be satisfied with the broken failures we see about us? Scientists dig in the earth to discover specimens of prehistoric man and then say, "This was a man." We say, "No." Man is something other than a skeleton found hidden in the hills. We have already been told that man has been crowned by the divine hand, but we do not see him crowned. The Scripture word says, "We see not yet all things put under him." There is hope in the words "not yet." Something else is promised. "Not yet" means "by and by." We are left indeed with more than hope, for the writer goes on to say: "We see not yet all things put under him. But we see Jesus." That is a strange way to reason. Surely that is a strange conclusion. Is there any real connection to the argument: "We see not yet all things put under him. But we see Jesus"? That is a strange way to argue. We do not see man crowned, but we see Jesus. Is there any hope there? Is there any prophecy there? Is there any salvation there? Surely there is. We see not yet all things subjected to him, but we see Jesus; and Jesus is a man, and we see him crowned and glorified.

You say one robin does not make a summer. Are you so sure

of that? If there is one robin, others will follow and summer will soon be here. You say one flower does not make a spring. Are you so sure of that? If we see one flower breaking through the sod, even though the snow is still on the ground, we know that there will be others and that soon the garden will be full of bloom. What one flower and one robin are to the springtime and the summer, Jesus is to our humanity. We see not yet all men crowned, but we see Jesus. We see him and he is crowned with glory and honor. He is not some skeleton specimen of a dead and ancient past, but the prototype and goal of all mankind, and in his train the generations follow.

And what he is, those who follow him must become. We can endorse only what Jesus would endorse. What does this mean? It means that there is something else. Jesus is not only our example, he is our empowerment. He not only champions manhood in himself, he champions it in us: "In that he himself hath suffered being tempted, he is able to succor them that are tempted." If Christ only challenged us as an example, he would be, as he indeed is, our condemnation. It would be like placing the work of Phidias before an amateur and commanding him to do likewise. Jesus is more than specimen. He is Saviour and Lord. What he is he will help us to be. He is more than pattern. He is power. He is more than example. He is spiritual energy. He is more than the model. He is more than the goal. He is the guide who leads us to the goal. He is not merely an illustration of what man may be at his best; he is the living inspiration of our life, the master light of all our seeing. The Greeks have a story of a god who entered the cold, crude marble and made it, as it were, live with the winsomeness and warmth of the divine life; and what the Greeks sought after, Christianity has realized.

This is Christianity's answer to the question, "What is man?" It is the answer that is desperately needed in our day. Man is more than the sum of his instincts and impulses. He is something other than his environment and his social conditions. He is something beyond the history that has helped to make him. He needs more than "a planned economy." There is something about him that is beyond nature, beyond heredity, beyond Communism, beyond the state. Not only does Christianity endorse the prophetic words of the Declaration of Independence that God has endowed man with certain inalienable rights, such as life, liberty, and the pursuit of happiness, but it opens up for man a boundless vista. It asserts that " now are we the sons of God, and it doth not yet appear what we shall be: but we know that, when he shall appear, we shall be like him; for we shall see him as he is."

14

The Christian Way to Think About Faith

"*Now faith is the substance of things hoped for, the evidence of things not seen.*" — Heb. 11:1.

In the ever remarkable story *Through the Looking-glass*, the White Queen says, " I'm just one hundred and one, five months and a day." Alice replied promptly, " I ca'n't believe *that!* " The Queen said: " Ca'n't you? Try again: draw a long breath, and shut your eyes." That is the way many people think regarding questions of belief and faith. But the Queen's attitude was not one of faith but of credulity. Faith is that quality of life which gives reality to things unseen; substance to things hoped for.

We live in a faith world. It is a world so constructed that it answers back and responds to faith. It is a world that echoes what we say and what we do. It says " Yes " when we say " Yes," and " No " when we say " No." To the cynic the world is cynical. To the tenderhearted the world is sweet and gentle, and to the toughhearted it is cruel and harsh.

The world answers back to our faith. It trusts when we trust it. It responds to our confidence. It says to the farmer, " Sow your seed "; to the aviator, " Spread your wings "; to the miner, " Sink your shaft "; to the sailor, " Hoist your sail "; to the engineer, " Swing your bridge "; to the scientist, " Trust your hypothesis ";

to the financier, " Make your investment "; to the explorer, " Follow the gleam." Faith is man's highest venture. The poet Whittier puts it thus: " The steps of faith fall on the seeming void and find the rock beneath." It is a " seeming void " on which we set our faith; beneath us, however, is the unseen reality, and faith gives it substance.

From this point of view, faith is the great creative force in the world. The psychologist tells us that it is according to our faith that we discover values. If we had faith as a grain of mustard seed, we could step out into victory. Captain Hadfield, in his suggestive essay *The Psychology of Power*, tells us clearly that faith creates power. Disappointment and discouragement lower the nervous and muscular forces by which we do our work in the world. As one who had charge of all the shell-shock and neurotic cases sent back to England from the First World War, Mr. Hadfield tells us how, under the form of suggestion, men were made strong or weak. In the normal waking condition a man has an average grip, he tells us, of one hundred and one pounds. When placed under hypnosis, the suggestion of weakness is given. A man who was strong and muscular was told that he had an arm of a little child and his grip slipped from one hundred and one pounds down to twenty-nine pounds. Then the suggestion of strength was given and his grip rose from one hundred and one pounds to one hundred and forty-two pounds. When men believed they were weak, they were weak. When they believed they were strong, they were strong. According to their faith it was done unto them.

We should get along far better in life if we had faith in those about us. Parents would succeed better with their children. Teachers would succeed better with their pupils. Preachers would succeed better with their congregations, if the element of faith prevailed. Faith gives substance and reality to the things for which we hope.

It is in this way that science works. Every laboratory is a temple of faith. Science throws a bridge out into empty space, into the unseen, and rests it upon the invisible. The scientist, of all men, is a man of faith, of imagination, dreaming his dreams of what may be and what must be, working with the invisible forces that co-operate with him and at last giving substance to that which was only hoped for. By faith, Newton discovered the law of gravitation. By faith, Herschel found the unknown planet Neptune moving through the vast expanse. By faith, Lowell saw the planet Pluto and died in faith, believing what he had not seen but which our generation has seen. By faith, Einstein found the law of relativity. By faith, two young Cambridge physicists found the secret of the atom. By faith, science believes that the world is made, not only of the things that appear, but of the things unseen.

Professor Eddington, the British physicist, suggests that the world should be divided into two parts: the part that can be measured by the foot rule of the ordinary mechanic or engineer; and the part that takes in all those immeasurable things which cannot be measured save by the golden measuring rod that is in the hands of the man who is the angel. There is a world of things and a world of thoughts, a world of science and a world of art, a world of substance and a world of values. And we cannot add up in one column all the values with which we come in contact. The scientist who demands that religion should submit to scientific tests is as mistaken as the theologian who demands that all science should be theologically interpreted. You cannot bring everything in the world under the same common denominator. The blind soldier who advertised his needs added up the interesting events of his life in one column. His advertisement ran: Battles, 7; wounds, 6; children, 8; total, 21. We smile at his calculations, but in our endeavor to force everything into the formula of some mechanistic hypothesis we are attempting the same impossible task.

It is so in religion. We reach out to find God and lo, he is there. True religion posits the truth that God is there. God himself is the great seeker. Pascal has put it in an unforgettable paradox, "Thou wouldst not be seeking Me, if thou hadst not found Me."

Faith in the realm of religion is not different from any other form of faith, except that its objective is different. Faith throws a bridge toward God and finds the divine Reality. We are wrong when we say that we must verify God and prove him first and then we will have faith in him. That is not the way knowledge is gained. It is not the way the scientist works. It is not the way the businessman works. Religion, like science, says, Throw out your bridge, trust your faith, put your hypothesis to the test, experiment with your dream and your hope, and by faith you will understand. Thomas Huxley said, "Sit down before nature as a little child or you will learn nothing." It is so with religion. If you come to religion as a cynic, with your clever prejudices, you will learn nothing. "The secret of the Lord is with them that fear him." The truth of God, like the truth of nature is found only by reverent seekers. Sit down before God as a little child and listen and learn. Throw out your bridge toward the unseen. Others have done it, and life is full of men and women and little children who, by faith, find God real. Will you sit down before the fact of Christ? Will you take the story of his life and read it reverently and let it speak to you its message?

The future is with men of faith. There is a striking monument to General Gordon outside the city of Khartoum in Egypt. It is a statue of Gordon sitting on a dromedary, and his face is toward the desert. A visitor one day, looking at it, said to the guide, "The face should be toward the city, toward the Nile from whence re-enforcements were to come to his relief." "No, sir," said the Arab, "he is not looking toward the city, not toward the Nile, but toward the desert, toward the Sudan, for which he died. He is waiting, sir, for the morning to dawn." That is the attitude of faith. To him who has faith to look across the desert and through the darkness, the morning light is sure to break.

15

The Christian Way to Think About Forgiveness

"*If we confess our sins, he is faithful and just to forgive us our sins, and to cleanse us from all unrighteousness.*" — I John 1:9.

THE judge on the bench recognizes that the best of men in a crisis may fail. The physician sees human nature slipping and failing behind the disease which he seeks to cure. The social worker understands that behind poverty and destitution the shadow of sin is recognized. The minister meets it everywhere in his work. The banker is conscious of its presence as he handles the securities that pass from hand to hand. In the words of Carlyle: "There is ever a dark spot in our sunshine. It is even, as I said, a shadow of ourselves." What, then, is the interpretation of this "dark spot"?

The psychologist tells us that it is a remnant, a leftover, an inner conflict which continues because of our inheritance from the jungle. It is a call of the wild echoing the animal inheritance which is ours. But that is not an adequate interpretation, for there is nothing sinful whatever about animal life. There is nothing sinful about the jungle. There is nothing sinful about immaturity. Animal passions are clean and pure and have nothing whatever to do with the deceptiveness and trickiness of human nature. The strange element that is in human nature does not belong to the physical but to the soul. It is something that concerns me. It is something I have said or done which I need not have said or done. It is an attitude that brings regret and remorse and shame so that the soul of man cries out, "My sin is greater than I can bear." It is an inner conflict of the soul in which there seems to be a dual personality that is not and cannot be at peace. The soul has it within its own power to give consent or to withhold it. I could have said "No," but I said "Yes"; I could have said "Yes," but I said "No." It is an inner act. It is something spiritual. The flesh and the body and the physical have nothing to do with it. It is the consent of my soul. It is my personal commitment.

In Robert Louis Stevenson's story, Mr. Hyde destroys Dr. Jekyll. It is the evil that crowds out the good. It is the flesh that destroys the spirit. The great Bible scholar Dr. George Adam Smith has said that for that reason he could think of hell, not as a place of fire, but as a condition where the fire has burned itself out and only the cold, barren waste, where everything has turned to ashes, remains. When the soul says "Yes" to God, there is a return to the soul's true life. Made in the image of God, the human soul is restless till it finds God, and only when the prayer is offered, "Not my will, but thine, be done," is there victory. This is the achievement of Christ. He came to save his people from their sins. He came to give them victory over themselves. He came to break down "the middle wall of partition" in our own lives and to create a new man, a new creature complete, united, whole. Across the ages we hear him say, "Wilt thou be made whole?" When we throw ourselves upon him, we become one in him. We are no longer dual personalities fighting within ourselves, divided, looking this way and that, living a Saturday and Sunday sort of life; but we become personalities that are at peace with themselves, that have achieved victory and that are able to act righteously, to say "Yes" to God. That is what we mean when we stand up and say, "I believe in the forgiveness of sins."

Let us, however, look at that statement a little more closely. What do we really mean when we say, "I believe in the forgiveness of sins"? If it means that the consequences and penalties and punishments of sin are wiped out, then we will demur. That is not true to reality or to experience. The consequences of sin are what they are and will be what they are. The bitter word is spoken and cannot be recalled.

> "Boys flying kites haul in their white-winged birds;
> You can't do that way when you're flying words. . . .
> Thoughts unexpressed may sometimes fall back dead;

But God himself can't kill them when they're said."
—From "The First Settler's Story," by Will Carleton.

The fatal poison is administered and it cannot be removed. The estrangement has taken place. The evil has been done.

"The Moving Finger writes; and, having writ,
Moves on: nor all your Piety nor Wit
Shall lure it back to cancel half a Line,
Nor all your Tears wash out a Word of it."
—From "The Rubáiyát of Omar Khayyám," trans. by Edward FitzGerald.

The wild oats are sown. "Whatsoever a man soweth, that shall he also reap." Even the reformed drunkard has permanently hurt his children and probably ruined his own health. The restored prodigal comes back to live with his memories and his shame. It is true, indeed, that God can do much to restore a forgiven life to health and happiness. The promise is that God will restore the years that the locusts have eaten, that he will repair the desolation of former generations. But the legacy and penalty of evil remain and the debts that may have accumulated must at last be paid.

Forgiveness, though, is something vaster, more wonderful, more amazing than that. Forgiveness has reference, not to acts merely, but to attitudes; not to particular deeds so much as to permanent relationships. True forgiveness speaks of renewed trust. It involves restoration of friendship. It brings about reconciliation. It restores confidence. It takes away all sense of estrangement and establishes a new relationship upon the rock foundations of trust and confidence. You will see how this is so in your dealing with your children. Forgiveness means the renewed kiss of affection, the restoration to favor even though there may be punishment and penalty required. That is what forgiveness in God means. It is God's new trust in the soul. It is God's new faith expressed in his willingness to trust us. God trusts us anew. He believes in us. He hopes for us. He puts responsibility again upon us. It was forgiveness that Jesus extended to Peter when he said, "'Simon, Simon, behold, Satan hath desired to have you, that he may sift you as wheat: but I have prayed for thee, that thy faith fail not: and when thou art converted' — then I have something for you to do for men. You must come back into the apostolic circle and minister to thy brethren."

It is forgiveness we hear spoken in the glad experience of Isaiah, where we find him in the presence of burning holiness crying out, "I am a man of unclean lips, and I dwell in the midst of a people of unclean lips." Then we read that the angel, touching his lips with burning fire, said, "Lo, this hath touched thy lips; and thine iniquity is taken away, and thy sin purged." Then we find restoration and renewal of trust, and in answer to the challenge, "Whom shall I send, and who will go for us?" the prophet, redeemed from sin, responds, "Here am I; send me." It is Jesus saying to the penitent prodigal, who had come home with the confession upon his lips, "Father, I have sinned against heaven," "Bring forth the best robe, and put it on him." And the house is relighted, the music is heard again, and the joy of complete understanding and fellowship has been restored.

When others have lost faith in us, when we have lost faith in ourselves, God trusts us. He bids us stand upon our feet and look the world in the face, and in that forgiveness we find hope, new confidence, new life even though there be "memories that bless — and burn!"

There is a vast difference between the fear of consequences that follows sin and the friendship of reconciliation. How is this done? Well, that is the gospel. It is done by God giving himself to us. How greatly he gives himself to us in Christ, in his life, in his cross and in his living presence! "Lo, I am with you alway, even unto the end." It is the love of God that redeems, that awakens within us new desires, new hopes, new aspirations, and a new response to holiness. In Owen Wister's book *The Virginian*, the uncultured cowboy who had been lifted up by human love said, "It was neither preaching nor praying that made a better man of me, but one or two people who believed in me better than I deserved and I hated to disappoint them." That is the story of God's trust in us. The eternal God thinks better of us than we deserve, and we are pledged not to disappoint him. How do we know that? We know that when we stand in the presence of Jesus, who gave himself for us and for our salvation. We know it when we stand beside his cross, from which he speaks forgiveness. He refuses the penalty. He shuts the door on enmity and opens the door to reconciliation, to the renewal of trust, and a new confidence in ourselves and in God's eternal love.

16

The Christian Way to Think About the Life to Come

"*And if I go and prepare a place for you, I will come again, and receive you unto myself; that where I am, there ye may be also.*"
—John 14:3.

THE idea of immortality is not a distinctly Christian idea but is a common hope of all religions. In Christianity, however, the idea takes on new significance. In other religions it is a vague, shadowy life. Jesus made it real when he said to the thief on the cross, "To-day shalt thou be with me in paradise." There would be no interval between death and heaven. There would be no sleep in the grave. When we leave life, we enter with him into life eternal. Richard Baxter wrote some true words:

"My knowledge of that life is small,
The eye of faith is dim;
But 'tis enough that Christ knows all,
And I shall be with Him."
—*From "Lord, It Belongs to My Care."*

Canon Liddon tells of an old sea captain who, recounting the wonders of a long, eventful life at sea, told a company of friends of the marvels that he had seen; and then pausing exclaimed, "But all this is nothing compared with what I yet expect to see!" His friends wondered at his statement, for he was past three score and ten. They asked him when and where he hoped to come upon his new discovery. Shading his eyes with his hand, he said, "The first five minutes after death." Can we think out the nature of that life which lies behind this life? What sort of life would life in the world to come be?

As Richard Baxter wrote of it in his verse, it would be a life of fellowship with Christ. His ideal would be our ideal. It would mean purity, patience, gentleness, kindness, charity. It would mean, above all, that to be with him would be to have fellowship in his meekness and his lowliness of heart. Otherwise, it would mean that we would be ill at ease, restless, and self-condemned. In the presence of Jesus, Judas had all the experience of being in hell. Heaven must be within a man before he can be in heaven. Without holiness no man can see God, and to be with Jesus is to have fellowship with him, in the loveliness and beauty of a holy life.

Nothing else can make heaven for you and for me. No change of place or scene is sufficient and the life that now is becomes the opportunity of all opportunities. What is it that we are doing in these fast passing days of ours? We are buying and selling and making merchandise of our time, forgetting perhaps that the only thing that lives on after the stars have died down is the soul, which was made in the image of God and for fellowship with him. This is what is behind the confession of Victor Hugo: "I feel within myself the future life. I am rising I know toward the sky. The sunshine is over my head. Heaven lights me with the reflection of unknown worlds. You say the soul is nothing but the result of bodily powers. Why then is my soul more luminous when my bodily powers begin to fail? Winter is on my head and eternal spring is in my heart. The nearer I approach the end the plainer I hear around me the immortal symphonies of the worlds which invite me. It is marvelous, yet simple. It is a fairy tale and yet it is history. For half a century I have been writing my thoughts in prose, verse, history, philosophy, drama, romance, tradition, satire, ode, song; I have tried all. But I feel that I have not said the thousandth part of what is in me. When I go down to the grave, I can say like so many others: 'I have finished my day's work,' but I cannot say, 'I have finished my life.' My day's work will begin the next morning. The tomb is not a blind alley — it is a thoroughfare. It closes in the twilight to open in the dawn. My work is only beginning. My work is hardly above the foundations. I would be glad to see it mounting and mounting forever. The thirst for the infinite proves infinity."

Furthermore, the life to come will mean a fellowship with Christ in service. To be with him means to be with him in the work and mission of his life. Could you think of Jesus otherwise than as active and still busy about the things of his Father? Sometimes we sing, "All His Work Is Ended"; but there is a sense in which that cannot be true. If in the life to come we are to be with him, it is to be, not in a passive, indolent, colorless, stagnant life, but in the fellowship of a life of service, of missionary endeavor, and of progressive hope. Therefore, it is written deep into the story of the life to come that "his servants shall serve him: and they shall see his face."

When President Harper, of the University of Chicago, was lying at the point of death, he called into his room a few of his closest friends and asked them to pray with him. "Now let us talk with God," he said; "let us not be formal; let us be simple." After they had prayed with him, he prayed himself and the burden of his prayer was this: "And may there be for me a life beyond this life, and in that life may there be work to do, tasks to accomplish; and this I ask for Jesus' sake." The Spirit of God was leading his thought along right lines. There will be much work for all of us to do. The work of the world is not done when this mortal has put on immortality, but has only begun. The gates of the new life open to us new opportunities for service, new tasks to accomplish. How many who have passed over the margin have only started to live! There will be limitless time, time for all the unfinished tasks and unfulfilled hopes of life.

In his thought-provoking book *The Next Religion,* Israel Zangwill makes the mother who lost her boy say to the father, whose religious hope had died out of his heart: "And is there not time enough and space enough and power enough to set all these blunders straight? Are you not always talking of the infinities and the eternities? Are there not stars enough and universes enough, or do you think I cannot wait a million years and journey a million, million miles, if only it were to hear my boy say once again, 'Mother.' Jesus' word to us there as here will be, 'Follow me.'"

It is only in this way and along this line of thinking that we will give reality to the Christian hope and make it a motive power for present living. Oliver Wendell Holmes tells us that he would have a father go to the school where his boy is, and suddenly, taking him out of the school, say: "Now, my boy, the time has come when your education is finished, and you must come out into the world with me. All the wide, wonderful world is before you." And then, as the boy stood with open eyes, looking out upon life, he would have the father say to the boy: "Now, my boy, this is just like death. Death is leaving the old school, with its hard lessons and its perplexing problems and unanswered questions, and passing out into the fuller life, with its golden opportunities and its unlimited field of service." This is the Christian point of view, and it is a point of view that gives us comfort and at the same time gives us courage; and we need courage even more than we need comfort.

> "Some day the bell will sound,
> Some day my heart will bound,
> As with a shout, That school is out,
> And, lessons done, I homeward run."
> —*From "School Days," by Maltbie D. Babcock.*

Section Four

THE CHRISTIAN LIFE

17

How to Be a Christian

"*And it came to pass, that a whole year they assembled themselves with the church, and taught much people. And the disciples were called Christians first in Antioch.*" — Acts 11:26.

It is possible to trace the word "Christian" to within ten years of the death of Christ. It is an unusual and provocative word. It has a Hebrew significance, a Greek formation, and a Latin ending. Like the title over the cross, it was written in Hebrew, Greek, and Latin. We are told that the history of the world is written in the rocks. It is also true that the history of redemption is written in the languages of civilization. You do not need to go far into the past to find the place where the name of Jesus was introduced into the language of the Orient. It is possible, also, to trace our religion in the origin and use of this word "Christian" through English and Old English, through High and Low German, through Latin and Greek, back to within ten years of the crucifixion. What surer apologetic for the Christian faith could there be! In that fact we have a strong anchor for our faith and credible evidence of the truth of the gospel we profess. Deeper than any fossil hidden in the rocks is the truth of the revelation of God embedded in the common language of the people.

When we look at the name "Christian," we notice that the name was "a child of necessity." The followers of Jesus did not call themselves by that name. They were called Christians by other people. They called themselves by less distinctive titles. In one verse the commonest name of all was used to describe them: "The disciples were called Christians." They were *disciples*. That is the name we find most frequently in the Gospels. Jesus was their teacher. They were his scholars and belonged to his school. It was from his lips that they learned the great teaching concerning God and the destiny of the human soul. He was their way, their truth, and their life. But they were more than scholars. They trusted in him; and so they were called *believers.* Through the Epistles the music of that word, which reveals a personal friendship and the fidelity of a great devotion, is heard again and again. They were called *saints* — separated men and women, men and women who would not associate themselves with the vile customs of pagan times, men and women who endeavored to be pure in heart and body. As their numbers grew and their social order enlarged, they called themselves " brethren," for they were united by a bond that was as strong as death. These were the names by which they were known: disciples, believers, saints, brethren; and they took up those common words and consecrated them.

The name " Christian " was given to the followers of Jesus neither by themselves nor by the Jews, but by the Greek-speaking people of Antioch. It was a nickname, a byword, and it was given in derision and contempt. Wherever we meet this word in the New Testament there is a sting in it; there is reproach and ridicule. Peter in his day said to his brethren: " Let none of you suffer as a murderer, or as a thief, or as an evildoer, or as a busybody in other men's matters. Yet if any man suffer as a Christian, let him not be ashamed." There you have the followers of Jesus classified in the thought of that time: thieves, evildoers, meddlers in other men's matters, " *Christians.*"

The name was " a child of necessity." A distinctive name was given to designate a new species. The people of Antioch had many names in their resourceful language but they had no name to cover this type of character. They had Greeks and Romans and Jews and Gentiles and Samaritans and pagans in that cosmopolitan city of Syria, but they had no name for these people among whom there was no room for such distinctions as Jew and Greek, bond and free, Barbarian and Scythian. New people, like new thoughts and ideas and things, demand new names. When the electrical age came in, a whole family of new names was born. When the age of science came in, a new dictionary had to be prepared. And this new manhood and womanhood had not hitherto been classified. These people did things, said things, lived things — lived things hitherto unheard of in the history of the world. They lived purity — purity of a new order, purity of thought and feeling. They lived forgiveness — forgiveness of a new kind, forgiveness for friend and foe alike. They lived love — love of a new order, love for all the world, for bond and free, rich and poor. They lived humility — humility new to the world, humility that was a reproach to the people, humility that made a friend of poverty and of workingmen and of slaves. These were the ideas they preached and taught and lived and glorified until they produced a new type of manhood and womanhood after the likeness of Jesus. When persecution and epidemic broke out at Carthage and the great and the wealthy fled in terror, Cyprian, the bishop of the church, said, "Now let us overcome evil with good"; and while friends and relatives left the city in dismay, the Christians labored on in their services of comfort and healing.

And this is what I am thinking about. I am wondering whether, if we were to lose the name today, were to lose it as Hermas lost the great word in the story of Henry van Dyke's *The Lost Word*, we would by our lives, by our conduct, and by our character re-create the necessity for a new name because of a distinctive type of character. Years ago Strauss published an article entitled "Are We Yet Christians?"; and the question is still provoking. Because of your Christian character would the men in your town need a new name by which to describe you? Because of the unselfishness of your disposition and the winsomeness of your character would you, who mingle in the social circles of the city, both claim and require the designation of a new name? Does your life demand the continuation of a distinctive name or must you wear a badge and recite a creed and herald your allegiance in order to be known as a Christian? Are we Christians when men and women across the seas tell the gospel story while we spend money for that which is not bread? Are we Christians when we lack the power to purify our commercial and civic and national life?

In a remarkable study of the life of Christ, *The Jesus of History*, the author, T. R. Glover, of Cambridge, says: "The Christian proclaimed a war of religion in which there shall be no compromise and no peace, till Christ is Lord of all; the thing shall be fought out to the bitter end. And it has been. He was resolved that the old gods should go; and they have gone. How was it done? Here we touch what I think one of the greatest wonders that history has to show. How did the Church do it? If I may invent or adapt three words, the Christian 'out-lived' the pagan, 'out-died' him, and 'out-thought' him. . . . The old religion crumbled and fell, beaten in thought, in morals, in life, in death. And by and by the only name for it was paganism, the religion of the back-country village, of the out-of-the-way places. Christ had conquered."

That victory of the Early Church is our challenge, for their God is our God and his Spirit still broods over all. In the surging centers of our commercial life, in New York, in Chicago, in Baltimore, in Pittsburgh, the challenging opportunity of the present is ours to demonstrate the transforming power of the gospel; and in the spirit of Him whom having not seen we love to bring in the new day of sweetness and light, of love and good will. This is our challenge and this is our call as Christians.

18

How to Pray as a Christian

"*But thou, when thou prayest, enter into thy closet, and when thou hast shut thy door, pray to thy Father which is in secret; and thy Father which seeth in secret shall reward thee openly.*" — Matt. 6:6.

JESUS said to his disciples, "When ye pray." He did not say, "If ye pray." He presented no evidence to men that prayer was a scientific and an experimental fact. He never presented an apology for prayer. He took for granted that everywhere and always men sought after God, if haply they might find him. I take it that in the language of Jesus prayer is synonymous with faith and the desire to find religious reality. The greatest inquiry of the Christian heart is expressed in the words of the disciples' request to Jesus: "Lord, teach us to pray."

As we grow older, we know how we return to the simplicity of our childhood. And this is true in praying. Many a grown man discovers himself saying the words, "Jesus, tender Shepherd, hear me," and it is interesting to think that Jesus also found in the simplicity of prayer the best expression of his mind and heart. Little does a mother know when she teaches a little child to pray — seldom do we realize — how formative the early religious influences are in a child. Horace Bushnell has said that when a child reaches the age of three, we have done for that child almost half of what we shall be able to do. Long after a mother's hand is removed and her voice is no longer heard, thinking perhaps that her prayers have been unanswered and her ministry unavailing, a man grown to maturity returns to the simplicity and reality of his childlike faith, which through the busy years had been obscured. Welling up from the deep places of his life comes not only memory but faith, and on his lips are heard again the words of confession, "Our Father which art in heaven."

But there are difficulties in the experience of prayer. There are obstacles that often stand in the way of our desire to seek first-hand acquaintance with the unseen. For example, when we pray, we sometimes feel as if we were talking to ourselves. It is as though we were calling in a forest and no one was there. In all our seeking and in all our praying the sense of seeming unreality clings to us. Prayer becomes to us merely a monologue, a soliloquy, a meditation instead of a dialogue in which we listen for the voice of God to speak. If there is, however, any reality to prayer, there must be faith to believe that God himself will answer when we call. This is why silence is so essential in all true prayer. We find the listening attitude necessary in all the activities of the mind. The scientist learns nothing unless he listens and his soul is quiet. The painter sees nothing unless he listens and waits. The poet hears nothing unless his ears are tuned to the music of the beautiful. It is this waiting upon God, this silence, this listening that brings its own reward. Again and again we find Jesus speaking the word "Father" and finding the divine response swift and sure.

Another difficulty that faces us in prayer is the wandering mind. I suppose we have all experienced the fact that when we begin to pray, our minds go off to the ends of the earth and we find ourselves saying words and phrases and repeating hackneyed expressions without any sense of corresponding reality. We are like little children saying our prayers and letting our thoughts run riot through all the play experiences of the day.

It is no different in prayer, however, from what it is in other things. The power of attention is limited and it is very difficult for any one of us to concentrate over a long period of time. Let me make one or two suggestions that I believe would be helpful in this.

Here is the Bible. It is the greatest book of prayer in the world. Its language is never frayed, or meager, or shopworn.

Here is the hymnal. There are few dead lines in the hymnal. The words live on from generation to generation and come to us out of all the languages of the world with fresh and vital experiences of the saints of God. There are words and lines that never grow old and there are new and unfamiliar lines that give wings to prayer.

Here is the prayer book. The literature of prayer has grown enormously in our day, and every year fresh books of prayer are circulated by the thousands.

Best of all, here are your own feelings and thoughts and words. A good practice to follow is to take time to write on a piece of paper the prayer that your heart is yearning to say. Many have found in this practice a valuable help, and I think that Jesus must have been in the habit of doing something like this. He must have taken time to think out the lovely language and the great words of the Lord's Prayer and hid them away in his mind before he ever gave expression to them.

It would be foolish to deny that there is such a thing as spontaneous prayer. All true prayer is, in a sense, spontaneous. At the same time it is not likely that we shall give expression to that which has not first been born of conviction. And in this most of us need help. We need guidance. We need the experience of those who have labored long before us in the art of prayer. We need also to know that our faith rests on sure evidence and strong assurance. For this, the helps that I have suggested are often a valuable means in learning to pray.

A third difficulty that sometimes arises is when we seek to enter into a deeper experience of prayer. We feel at times the apparent failure and uselessness of prayer because nothing seems to happen. The prize is not awarded. The life is not saved. The burden is not lifted. We turn away, our souls inarticulate, feeling that we can pray and nothing will happen. I suppose every one of us has had that experience. We have left the sickroom, or the hospital, or the place of business, feeling that the world is empty and that we cry aloud when there is no answer but the echo of our own cry. Saint Paul had that experience when he asked that his burden — his thorn in the flesh — be removed and it was not. In time the only answer that came back to him was, "My grace is sufficient for thee." Well, that in itself is an answer.

Jesus had the same experience, and to it we return again and again when we think of our unanswered prayers. In the Garden he prayed three times the same agonizing prayer: "If it be possible, let this cup pass away from me." The cup did not pass away but was pressed, instead, to his lips, and he was compelled to drink it to the very bottom. Nevertheless, he kept on praying because he looked on prayer, not as a soliloquy or a meditation, but as a submission to the will of God, by means of which the divine energy was released for the accomplishment of God's purpose. It is a poor, sickly way to think of prayer as the winning of one's own way. No, it is not the winning of our way, but the victory of God's way, and it is just that victory which sometimes causes our soul's agony. More even than submission, prayer, at its best, is co-operation. Think of how Jesus said, "I and the Father are one." There is nothing abstract in this relationship. God is all that the philosophers have said he is. He is "the power that works for righteousness." He is the "inscrutable Unknown." But God is also "Father." He is a Person. He is a Spirit. When this truth becomes known, prayer becomes not merely a religious ritual but a personal necessity.

Is prayer the forgotten secret in your life? Is it that you are so sufficient that you do not need to pray? It should not be. It need not be. For prayer in its simplest form says, " Father, into thy hands I commend my spirit." Try it. Let your will co-operate with God's will and see if there are not " more things . . . wrought by prayer than this world dreams of."

19

How to Suffer as a Christian

" *And his disciples asked him, saying, Master, who did sin, this man, or his parents, that he was born blind?* " — John 9:2

A LITTLE imagination will let us see the situation in that humble home in Jerusalem. There is a thrill of expectancy of a new life coming. There is the gracious preparation for the welcome that will be extended. If it is a little boy, there will be clothes and school and synagogue to think about. Perhaps there are grandparents who feel that the new life will continue the family name and make the years blossom again into springtime. When the little child is born, joy and feasting, eating and drinking, merriment and congratulations are everywhere evident. After a few days, a few weeks of undisturbed happiness, suddenly one morning the mother looks into the eyes of her baby and there is a stifled sob as she discovers that her beautiful boy is blind. What word of comfort is there? The long years of darkness fall upon her and she lifts her face to the God of her fathers and says, " My God, . . . why hast thou forsaken me? " All the agony of the world is in that moment.

And the disciples, sensing the situation, immediately said, " Who did sin, this man, or his parents, that he was born blind? " That is still a rather common reaction to suffering. When there is sorrow or trouble or accident or a sudden revelation of some incurable disease or the loss of some loved one, we immediately want to know why. There was once a cartoon, entitled "The Triumph of the Zeppelin," in which was pictured a humble home. On the bed lay the body of a young woman who had been killed by a bomb dropped by the great ship. Beside the bed a young man and a little child stood, dazed with grief and pain; and the child is saying: "But why, Father? Mother has done nothing wrong." It is an old and familiar reaction to say that somewhere sin has been at work. Somehow or other there is an instinct in all of us which confirms the opinion that punishment is the fruit of wrongdoing. We meet it in the experiences of life every day. If some tragedy happens, people say, "What have I done to deserve this?" There is, of course, a measure of truth in this question, for sin eventually does bring forth its own fatal fruit. This was the problem presented in The Book of Job. His friends said that Job suffered because he sinned. But Job would not accept that interpretation, and, when the story ends, Job was justified by God for his refusal. Job, however, lived before the cross of Christ and he did not know the real secret.

Jesus definitely discredited the position that suffering was the result of sin. In the Oriental dogma of the karma it is stated that sin can work itself out through thousands or millions of reincarnations unto the time when blessedness is at last achieved and the soul enters into a world of nothingness. Jesus answered quite frankly, "Neither hath this man sinned, nor his parents." It is not an adequate explanation to say that men suffer because they have sinned. When the tower in Siloam fell and killed eighteen people, Jesus quickly replied: "Think ye that they were sinners above all men . . . ? I tell you, Nay."

The attitude of the disciples was one of curiosity. The attitude of Jesus was entirely different. The disciples approached the problem with the question, "Who did sin?" They raised the question out of intellectual curiosity. But Jesus asked no such question. He said, "Neither hath this man sinned, nor his parents: but that the works of God should be made manifest in him." That statement, let us understand, does not mean that the man was born and destined to be blind so that this miracle of healing could be exhibited. Rather, said Jesus, understand that in the suffering of this young lad there is the chance for the purpose of God and will of God to be revealed in him. The disciples asked, "Why?" We wonder why. Why do men suffer? Why was the baby born blind? Why did the tragedy happen? Why did the hidden disease lay hold upon him? Thousands of men and women and little children live their lives in agelong suffering — shut-ins, prisoners in homes and hospitals. When they ask the question, Why?, what has Jesus to say? Listen to his answer. He says, in effect, "Do not ask why men suffer or where suffering comes from; but ask, rather, since it is here, What are we going to do about it?" Whatever questions we may have about it — and we may have many — there is at least this certainty. Suffering is a fact. It is a reality. It is no dream. It is no illusion. It is no fancy. It has entered life. It has darkened the corner of home and hearth. Do not, then, ask, "Why?" Ask, rather, "What can I do with this disappointing tragedy that has crossed my path?"

There are two things that can be done. We can resent it. We can refuse to accept the situation that we deplore. We can be rebels. We can become sour in our attitude. We can become cold and bitter and silent. This is often done. Men and women have turned away from God and Church and Christianity and all religion because they have rebelled against life and its experiences. They have fallen away and become cynical. That is not a good way. It was not Jesus' way. It makes us hard and irritable and only increases the pain we seek to ease. The years only laugh at our resentment. If you want to shut God out of your life, you can; and the universe will go on its way and you will become increasingly unhappy and bitter.

The other way to look at it is to accept what comes to us. We can take up our cross and say, "Not my will, but thine, be done." Suffering and pain and evil may not be of God's making but they are, nevertheless, under his control and remain subject to his guidance; and in the doing of his will, the discovery of his purpose for our lives, we shall find our peace. That is why we pray, "Thy will be done"; which is not submission but co-operation. Michelangelo looked on the block of fine Carrara marble which had been mutilated by a bungling sculptor and left in the quarry. He could have spent his time criticizing the man who had made a mess of things, and with good reason; but instead of that he made the very mutilation of the stone subservient to his own purpose and carved the inimitable figure of David the shepherd lad which has stood through time as a thing of beauty in the city of Florence. We cannot change the facts of life. They are thus and so, whether we like them or not; but it is in our power to use them so that the very things that are against us may turn to our advantage.

It was so in the experience of this child for whom everything worked out to his good. And we can see him standing in the midst of his opponents, championing truth and goodness and at last bowing in worship before his Lord. We are sure of it in relation to Saint Paul, who, coming through pain and suffering, shipwreck and imprisonment, was able to stand up and say, "I am persuaded, that neither death, nor life, nor angels, nor principalities, nor powers, nor things present, nor things to come, nor height, nor depth, nor any other creature, shall be able to separate us from the love of God." We see it, above all, in the life of our Lord, who did no sin but upon whom the cross was laid. If any man had a right to turn away from faith in the goodness of God, it was Jesus; and yet on the cross, asking the unanswered question, Why?, he bowed his head and said, "Father, into thy hands I commend my spirit."

What better answer could be given to our question, "Why do men suffer?" Suffering is a reality. Pain is a mystery. It is ours, not to spend our strength in intellectual curiosity concerning its origin, but, rather, to accept it and to discover what God has in it for us. To come through the battle with all the flags flying—that is victory!

20

How to Endure Temptation as a Christian

"*And when the tempter came to him, he said, If thou be the Son of God, command that these stones be made bread.*" — Matt. 4:3.

THE painting most suggestive of the temptation of our Lord in the wilderness is that by Cornicelius, a German artist of the nineteenth century. His painting, *Christ Tempted by Satan*, finished in 1888, is or was in the Berlin National Gallery. It consists chiefly of a remarkable portrait of the face of our Lord. His eyes are red with long sleeplessness and watching. His hair is blown about by the wind of the wilderness. Behind him in the shadow but not seen by him is an outline form of the tempter who, with raised hands, is about to place a crown upon his head. It is the face of Christ that is the remarkable thing about this picture, and the crown suggestive of world power that the tempter would place on his head. There is no suggestion here of a physical conflict, but only of a face that is deep in thought, and of a mind that has gone through a tremendous mental and moral struggle. It is the portrait of a religious experience. The hands of Christ clasp each other and not the crown, and you can see the agony that has taken place through forty days while Jesus has thought his way out into the light of victory.

We are not in the dark as to what that conflict was. Power was his. Divine power without limit had been granted him. The Holy Spirit had been given to him without measure. He had power over the forces of life and over the lives of men. What should he do with it? How should he use it? "If thou be the Son of God," says the tempter, "take this path, achieve this goal, climb these steps and enter into thy kingdom." It is a question that has to do with his lifework, with his career, with his vocation in the world.

It is similar to the test that comes to all young men and women on the threshold of their life's desires. Here is a young man who is in college. He is about to graduate. He has prepared himself and knows that he possesses certain power, certain knowledge, certain talent; and he faces life with the questions on his lips: "What shall I do with my life? How shall I invest my ability?" All young men and women who think seriously come face to face at some time with the shadow of a crown. They are tempted to fall down and worship the ways of the world in order to come into the possession of the kingdom of this world.

That is the temptation. That is the only temptation, and the artist has rightly interpreted the conflict that possessed the soul of Jesus. Will it be a life that counts for self and for world prestige, or will it be a life that loses itself in service to others? Will it be a crown that stands for force or shall it be a cross that stands for love? There is no other temptation. Though it is possessed of the same spirit, it takes many forms. It presented itself to Jesus in three changing aspects, but through all the changing aspects it is the same temptation. The problem presented to Jesus was in a word this: How can I attract these careless, self-centered, idle, busy people? How can I win them?

Jesus was tempted to use his power in making bread out of the stones at his feet. "If thou be the Son of God," said the tempter, "command that these stones be made bread" — if you are the Son of God, if that is really what you are, if you have divine power, if you are conscious of miraculous endowment, satisfy your hunger with bread, here and now. Translated out of the symbolic, the temptation to Jesus was to put the emphasis on the external and the material side of life. Build, says the tempter, on substantial reality. Begin first with the body, and having administered to the body then, and then only, think of the soul. Deal with physical necessities, for they are fundamental. Like Moses, give the people bread. Feed them with manna, satisfy the hunger of the multitude, become an economic messiah and build a new social order on a well-fed and physically satisfied humanity.

The temptation repeated itself and returned in another form. The suggestion came that Jesus should make a spectacular entrance into the life of the nation, leap from the pinnacle of the Temple and appear in the Temple courts as if borne upon angels' wings. "If you are the Son of God, if that is what you really are, if all power is given unto you, if miraculous endowment is your possession, if God is indeed your Heavenly Father, cast yourself down, and he will give his angels charge over you." If you can trust God for bread, then trust him for everything. Trust God to the limit. Let God do it. Force the issue and compel God to provide success.

It is the same temptation in another dress. It is the temptation to put the emphasis of life on the external and the spectacular. It is the temptation to follow the path of the miraculous and to leave the more difficult path of the natural. The worldly way is the way of the spectacular and the miraculous. The divine way is the way of the normal and the natural.

The hardest test, however, was still to come. A third time the temptation returned to Jesus. It was the same temptation in another guise. The vast kingdoms of the world stretched before him in panoramic array, and he was offered the throne of the world if he would follow the path to world power. "If you are the Son of God, if all power has been given unto you, if you are the Messiah, the King, then fall down and worship me and all the kingdoms of the world shall be yours." We know what that means. Many a man has been led into a high mountain and shown the kingdoms of this world and the glory of them. Mohammed had that experience and bowed down and entered into world power. The great war lords of history have had that experience — Caesar and Cyrus and Napoleon and William the Kaiser and Hitler and Mussolini. They all saw the shadow of a crown and raised it to their heads and bowed in worship before the great forces of this world.

The three temptations are one temptation and the temptation continued with him through his ministry and to his cross. It returned to him again when he hung upon the cross and the people cried, "'If thou be the Son of God, come down from the cross'; and we will believe thee." Jesus, however, did not come down. He had fought out the battle and chose the way of the cross. There is no other way to endure the crisis of temptation. There is no easy way, no short cut. The way out is by way of affliction — spiritual affliction! Always spirit must struggle against flesh. Always the unselfish must fight against the selfish.

Is there someone now who dares to say that Jesus made a mistake? Will anyone come forward and assert that Jesus should not have done what he did? No, there is no one who will say that. And if this great crisis in the life of Jesus is to do us any good, then we must face the question for ourselves. It matters little whether we are carpenters or capitalists or laborers, whether we belong to the rich or the poor, the educated or the unlearned, whether we are college graduates or belong to the rank and file, we cannot escape the challenge either to fall down and worship the world or to rise up and follow Christ.

21

How to Be Content as a Christian

"*Not that I speak in respect of want: for I have learned, in whatsoever state I am, therewith to be content.*" — Phil. 4:11.

I HAVE learned, in whatsoever state I am, therewith to be content." No — not satisfied, not content with things as they are, but master of things! There is a contentment that is born of the devil. Thousands are contented who ought to be disturbed out of their contentment and made restless and dissatisfied. The word used here — the only place it is used in the New Testament — means something else. It means undefeated. It means self-sufficient. With his back to the wall, Paul means to say that circumstances have not mastered him. He is master of his fate. He is captain of his soul.

Call to mind the situation out of which these words came. This is no sky-blue optimist who is speaking high-sounding words in the garden of life. This man is mature. The best part of his life is behind him. At sixty-five a man has a right to speak about himself. He is poor, terribly poor, so poor that he had to accept charity from his friends at Philippi who had ministered to his necessity. This letter was written to thank them for their kindness to him. He had received their charity not as right but with gratitude.

Furthermore, he was in prison; not in a modern concentration camp, but in a Roman prison, chained to a Roman soldier. How could he be content? He was a man of the open road, of God's out of doors, and there was work calling him. It was in these circumstances that he said, "I have learned, in whatsoever state I am, therewith to be content." We think of Napoleon standing with his hands behind his back, as he is often pictured, looking out over the sea from his prison in St. Helena and thinking of empires that once were his. He is restless, unhappy, chafing at fortune, bitter of soul, disillusioned. He was neither master of himself nor of his circumstances. He had not learned the secret. His biography would never suggest this high-souled self-sufficiency of the apostle.

Paul states that neither poverty nor wealth, neither success nor failure, neither the ups nor the downs of life, drove him from his course. "I know both how to be abased, and I know how to abound. . . . I am instructed both to be full and to be hungry, both to abound and suffer need." Think of that. He knew how to abound, how to carry success, how to be rich. Once he had had wealth, but it did not spoil him. He had learned how to deal with money. How few there are who have learned the secret of how to be rich. Riches spoil men. They cause them to be self-satisfied and proud. Truly few men know how to be rich. Paul knew also how to be poor and to keep his self-respect. It is more difficult to be poor and not be a pauper today than ever before in history. People become bitter and revengeful when poverty comes. They blame their poverty upon someone and lose their faith in God. But there are people who, like Saint Paul, know how to be poor and to keep their self-respect. It is a secret worth learning.

How did Paul learn the secret? He says that he did learn it. The word he uses is meaningful. He says that he was initiated into the secret. It is the word used when a man is initiated into a fraternity or a secret order. Paul claimed that he had been initiated into the secret of mastery. He had learned the secret from Jesus. When he dedicated his life to Christ, the will of Christ became his will. Jesus knew how to be poor. His cradle was borrowed. He had no place to lay his head. He died naked upon the cross. But poverty did not spoil his life or make him envious of the wealth of others. He knew how to be rich. " Though he was rich, yet for your sakes he became poor." When Christ became his master, Paul learned from Jesus three important triumphant principles.

First, he learned from Jesus *a new and true philosophy of life.* His motto was, " Rejoice in the Lord." He learned how to think in inclusive terms. No man can plant his feet firmly without first being sure that he is not standing on a fog bank. The greatest need of the modern world is a working philosophy of life, and Paul learned that philosophy at the feet of Jesus. Charles Spurgeon tells of a farmer who had on the weather vane of his barn the motto, " God is love." He was asked if the motto was intended to suggest that God is as changeable as the wind. " Oh, no! " said the farmer. " It means that whatever way the wind blows, God is love." That is the secret of being content, of a quiet heart, of self-mastery.

Secondly, Paul possessed, through Christ, *a new perspective of life.* His motto, oft-repeated, contains the words, " The Lord is at hand." Perspective is an artist's word. It calls for depth and distance and direction. Early art was superficial and revealed only a surface view. True art has depth and distance and reveals far-off vistas. We see a picture of woodland and a path leading off into the horizon. We see a picture of the sea and the limitless horizon that bids us dream of the land we do not see. True art has perspective; and what is life but the truest and highest of arts? The true life has depth and distance, and " believes in the centuries against the hours." Time is always on the side of truth, for a thousand years in God's sight are " but as yesterday, . . . and as a watch in the night." " God does not pay at the close of every day, but in the end he pays," said Anne of Austria to Richelieu. " He that soweth to the Spirit shall of the Spirit reap life everlasting." The man who has this hope can possess his soul in patience and say with the apostle, " The Lord is at hand."

Thirdly, Paul received from Jesus *a new psychology.* Jesus taught Paul how to think and what to think about. Was he thinking of his prison? of Nero's injustice? of the inevitable sentence of death? No, he was thinking of other things. He was thinking, not of defeat and death, but of victory. He was thinking, not of Nero on his throne, but of the eternal God. He was thinking, not of his enemies, but of his friends, who were even then ministering to his necessity and whose kindness had warmed his heart. Therein lies one of the secrets of self-mastery. We hear in our day a good deal about the power of mental suggestion and the influence of the subconscious thought. Paul long ago gave us the true principles of that philosophy, and he gave it adequate expression in unsurpassed language, "Whatsoever things are true, whatsoever things are honest, whatsoever things are just, whatsoever things are pure, whatsoever things are lovely, whatsoever things are of good report; if there be any virtue, and if there be any praise, think on these things."

So far as the record goes, Nero is gone and the Roman Empire has gone, the gladiators and lictors, and the arena itself, have all gone; and here we are taking new heart and courage from Paul's faith and courage, who defied time to defeat him or circumstances to overwhelm him.

Section Five

THE CHRISTIAN SERVICE

22

Christian and Pagan Ideologies

"And we know that all things work together for good to them that love God, to them who are the called according to his purpose."
— Rom. 8:28.

WOULD you be willing to say that the period through which we are now living is probably one of the most thoughtful periods in the history of the world? Notwithstanding the fact that there is much smugness and complacency among us, I think it is quite true that the whole world is in a thinking mood. Old things are passing away and the thinking of the world is being driven into strange new channels. That this is a fact is revealed in the creation of modern systems of thought, which we call ideologies. The word ideology means the science of ideas. It represents thinking that has been crystallized into a system. Any system of thought that seeks to explain the world can be rightly called an ideology, and the various ideologies that are prevalent today are attempts to answer the profound and serious questions of life; such as: What is the destiny of man? What is the world trying to do? Has history a meaning or is it just one thing after another? Any systematic effort to give an answer to these questions creates an ideology. When Macbeth, beaten and broken on the wheel of circumstances, exclaims in his agony that "Life's but a walking shadow, a poor player that struts and frets his hour upon the stage and then is heard no more: it is a tale told by an idiot, full of sound and fury, signifying nothing," he is giving expression to an interpretation, a philosophy, an ideology, an attitude of life.

What, then, are some of these new ideas, new philosophies, new ideologies, that seek to give us new interpretations about the meaning of life?

An ideology that has become prevalent during the last few years may be called *political.* We are told, and have been repeatedly told, that history is the forward push of life toward the freedom of man. Democracy is the end toward which history moves. Freedom, said Epictetus long ago, is "the right to live as we wish," and is that not the end for which we strive? The meaning of history, so we're told, is the perfection of political liberty. History is the record of the world that has moved out of slavery into freedom. One of the most memorable chapters in the record book of humanity is the story of the struggle for freedom, inspiring the noblest self-sacrifice and claiming the highest loyalties. And yet today freedom fights with its back to the wall. Each new day records how some hard-won freedom has been taken away. There is less freedom in America. There is more slavery in Europe. Instead of man's forging on and up to newer heights, he seems to be going down and down into newer forms of bondage. The ideology of freedom has fallen upon evil days.

A system of ideas that is concentrated along *biological* lines has created an ideology that believes in race and blood. This interpretation of life was a predominant factor in the thinking of the German Nazi regime. There is nothing new about it. It is as old as the Bible. Sometimes we see it expressed in certain anti-Semitic tendencies. Sometimes it comes out in our dealings between Negro and White or Asian and European. The purpose of such an ideology as this is to bring to flower a race of supermen, superior men to whom all other men must bow in deference. But in the light of our Christian teaching, to think of anything like a superior race or a superior man or a superior nation is to think in ignorance and foolishness.

There is yet another ideology, which roots itself in *economics* and proclaims that the history of mankind is a class struggle. It is a theory popularized by Communism. We are told that when the domination of the working class becomes secure, then the end and meaning of history will be made clear. But we are beginning to see that there is something much more fundamental, something much more at stake, than the pitting of class against class. It is not a part of our way of life to believe that history moves toward the supremacy of one class and to the extinction of another class. Such an interpretation of facts fails to explain the meaning that lies deep at the heart of life and of history.

Over against these pagan ideologies which have torn our world asunder, there is what we may call the Christian ideology. There is a Christian way of looking at life. There is a Christian interpretation of history. What is it? What are the ideas that are crystallized in the teaching of Jesus and brought into focus by his life and death and resurrection? Suppose we simplify it and give a familiar answer and yet one of the most profound testimonies in the Bible: "We know that all things work together for good to them that love God, to them who are the called according to his purpose." Is that a trustworthy interpretation or merely superficial optimism? Saint Paul does not argue about it. He states it as a fact, and he is not stating anything in the abstract. He is not saying that everything will come out all right for everybody. We know that is not true. We know only too well how life can fall apart.

The ideology that is presented here is personal and limited. It is confined to them that love God. It asserts that to them that love God all things, good and evil, failures and successes, work out to a satisfactory conclusion. That is worth thinking about. The man who loves God, who puts God in the center of his life, interprets life and history and events from a totally different point of view from the man who does not in any way relate his life to God. The same events spell out different destinies to different men. A recent writer tells of two families in the same town, each of which lost in the same accident an only son. One boy belonged to the home of the minister of the village, and the other was the son of a worldly family who lived apparently without God. A neighbor boy of twelve was talking about the tragedy to his mother and said: "Mother, it isn't so hard on the minister and his wife, for they know what to do. But these other people don't know what to do." So it is. Disease, failure, death mean different things to different people.

In the statement that he has given us Paul seems to be saying something like this: The world in which our lot is cast is a world of suffering. The whole created world groans, as if in pain; and we too struggle, seeking redemption and release. We do not struggle in vain, however, but in hope; for we look for the redemption that is promised according to the will of God. Since we know who God is, we know that all things will work out to our advantage according to his purpose for us, and his purpose is to bring us into fellowship with Christ, to be made perfect in him, and therefore we have this confidence that "neither death, nor life, nor angels, nor principalities, nor powers, nor things present, nor things to come, nor height, nor depth, nor any other creature, shall be able to separate us from the love of God, which is in Christ Jesus our Lord."

This, then, is the Christian interpretation of life, the Christian ideology. It interprets history as moving on, not to the building of a civilization, not to the creation of industry or culture or art, but to the making of personal character. Suppose we ask a question: What is the greatest thing in our world? If a visitor from another planet came and asked to be shown around our world, what would we point out as of the highest worth? Where would we take our visitor? What would we show him? Would we show him our steel plants, our aluminum plants, our factories and furnaces? Would we take him to see our universities and churches? Would he like to see our radios and airplanes? We could, of course, speak of Shakespeare and Homer and Wagner and Raphael. And after all this, the visitor might say: "Well, you have had a long history with lots of opportunity. What have you in the world that is of supreme value?" An English poet has tried to answer that question. What is the distinction of this world of ours among all the circling planets and fixed stars of the boundless universe? This is what the poet answers:

> "With this ambiguous earth
> His dealings have been told us. These abide:
> The signal to a maid, the human birth,
> The lesson, and the young Man crucified."
>
> — *From "Christ in the Universe," by Alice Meynell.*

The biggest and best thing about this world is that here a "young Man crucified" lived his life in perfect virtue. The fact that Jesus Christ was born on this planet, lived his life here, died here and rose again, is the one great distinguishing event that lifts this planet out of all comparison with the stars and suns in our vast universe. If this, then, is so, the thing that approaches this greatest of all happenings in our world is a man or a woman who in turn reflects the character of Christ. The New Testament clearly states that this is the purpose of life and history.

A perfect world is not needed to achieve the end set forth in the Christian ideology. It can be achieved in any situation. It does not need to wait on Utopia. What is needed is an endless world, and the one thing that these pagan ideologies do not take into account is this fact of immortality and eternity. Each of these pagan ideologies has its end in this world. Not so with the Christian ideology. It cannot end within the limits of this life. It needs eternity, for personality partakes of the life of God and moves on through the ages. A character in one of George Macdonald's stories cries out in frustration, "I do not see why God ever made me"; to which her friend replies: "God hasn't made you yet. He is making you and you don't like it."

Again and again in the New Testament we see the outreach into eternity. Say over to yourself this interpretation that Paul has set forth: "We know that all things work together for good to them that love God, to them who are the called according to his purpose. For whom he did foreknow, he also did predestinate to be conformed to the image of his Son, that he might be the firstborn among many brethren. Moreover, whom he did predestinate, them he also called: and whom he called, them he also justified: and whom he justified, them he also glorified." That is the ladder by which we ascend. These are the steps that lead on and up to the Mount of Vision. This is the end of the road, the victory of life, the final achievement of history. Higher than this no man can attain. This is something that transcends all pagan ideologies. What, then, shall we say to these things? What else but this, "If God be for us, who can be against us?"

23

The Greatest Need of America

"Blessed is the nation whose God is the Lord;
And the people whom he hath chosen for his own inheritance." — Ps. 33:12.

IN the opening sentence of an important biography on the life of Dwight L. Moody, the evangelist, the biographer Gamaliel Bradford, writing from the point of view of a man of letters, says: "Surely we may end as we began, with the insistence that God is the one supreme universal need of all humanity, and that need was never more pronounced than in America today." Would you agree with that analysis of America's need? If so, why? That is the question which we want to ask ourselves. Why does America today need God? Let us look at three suggestive answers.

First, America needs God today because of its unparalleled prosperity. We could speak of America's abounding resources, its increased foreign trade, its enlarged commerce, its expanding bank balances, its Gibraltarlike position in the markets of the world. We could say that there has never been a nation that has had the enormous wealth that America enjoys, or a nation that has enjoyed such unlimited luxury and so securely rides upon the top of the world as does America. And yet, on the other hand, if we were historians, we should quickly see that ease and luxury and wealth have never assured national continuity. History has only one story to tell and that is about the enervating effect of a comfortable and luxurious prosperity.

The great animals, the dinosaurs and the megalosaurs and the huge carnivorous lizards, at whose skeletons we look in wonder and alarm, were immune from harm and danger. They lived safely and luxuriously. Their lives were protected from injury by an impenetrable armor. They lived a fearless, self-satisfied, complacent, comfortable existence. But today they are extinct. Luxury and an easy life destroyed them; whereas, the animals that were alert to danger are still with us. What is true of individuals is true of nations. It is impossible to serve God and mammon, and mammon is just another name for money.

Secondly, America needs God as never before because life has become mechanized. The physical needs of man have developed more quickly than his spiritual appetite is able to absorb. The machine has expanded, but the man that drives the machine is still the same as he was before the machine age came in upon us. Instead of being the master of the machine, he is the slave of the machine which he has created. He is able to do more than his father did. The automobile has lengthened his legs. The airplane has lengthened his arms. The radio and telephone have extended his voice. The electric current has quickened his pulse. He is able to do more, to travel faster, to reach out farther than his father. Modern man belongs to a machine age and the machine is in high gear and in many hands it is out of control.

Who is going to control these released physical forces? Have we character enough to use them? A distinguished scientist has said: "Science has endowed man with the power of a superman, but his mind remains human, all too human. He is like a pauper come into a fortune, a laborer who has been put into the position of boss of the shop, a private promoted to command the regiment, a slave made the master of slaves. Man has had no training for such responsibilities as have now been thrust upon him. This new command of time and space, this mastery of unknown forces, this apparition of new perils, this entrance into untried fields, all these are too much for man of today." For these reasons we need to have our moral and mental sanity restored. We need a new moral adjustment to our enlarged physical environment. We need new spiritual endowment. We need God.

Thirdly, America needs God because of its present unlimited influence in the world. We are no longer a self-contained and self-sufficient people. We have far-reaching, entangling alliances with all the nations of the earth and our prosperity and happiness are bound up with the peoples of other lands. In a very real sense the world of tomorrow will be what America chooses to make it. We can make it an armed camp. We can make it an arena for naval competition. We can make it the scene of racial hatred and malicious mischief. On the other hand, we can make this world a palace of peace. We can make it a family of friendly nations. We are now struggling to make it so and we must not become impatient. We must endure to the end, and the nation that clings to God can and will endure. The day will come when a godless Russia will hold out its hands to a God-acknowledging America.

We do not know why nations rise and fall. But they do. Historians have pointed out that nations rise and fall in regular rhythmic intervals. Arnold Toynbee, the prominent historian, tells us there is only one chance for civilization to endure. Nations have fallen because of inward decay. They have committed moral suicide. America, to live, must lay hold upon the living God.

How can we lay hold upon God? For one thing, let men and women who seek high position in the nation publicly acknowledge God. Let them make some avowal of God's place in the life of our nation. In the second place, let us give our support to every institution that helps the nation to remember its dependence upon God. In the third place, let us refuse to have anything to do with any movement that seeks to crowd God out of our life and out of our institutions. In the fourth place, let us practice the presence of God in business and in our homes and in our schools. In the fifth place, let us each of us say to his own soul morning, noon, and night, "My soul, wait thou only upon God; for my expectation is from him."

24

The Prince of Peace

[WORLD ORDER SUNDAY]

"*To whom also Abraham gave a tenth part of all; first being by interpretation King of righteousness, and after that also King of Salem, which is, King of peace.*" — Heb. 7:2.

THERE can be no peace until there is righteousness. Uneasy lies the head where there is a guilty conscience. The paths of righteousness are beside the still waters. "The wicked are like the troubled sea, when it cannot rest, whose waters cast up mire and dirt. There is no peace, saith my God, to the wicked." Peace and a quiet heart are the fruit of a right life.

A friend was explaining an invention by means of which weak places in steel rails could be detected. It did not take long to see the importance and value of what had been worked out. Sand holes and air cavities, which often work themselves into the hidden places of a steel rail or girder, can make the product we trust defective and untrustworthy. With the help of this delicate instrument, used to pass smoothly over the steel, places of weakness are revealed, thus guaranteeing security. Inasmuch as peace and safety depend upon the strength of that steel construction across which we travel back and forth, so, as it is with steel, is it with the lives of men. Peace and security come through righteousness.

Peace is a by-product of righteousness. It is the fruit of a true life. In the peace and patience of a quiet heart Sir Walter Raleigh lay down to die, saying, "It matters not how the head lies if the heart is right." When his life was wrong, Paul struggled through the agony and trial described in the seventh chapter of Romans, torn with conflicting passions, flung back against the storm, crying in the night of his helplessness, "O wretched man that I am!" When his life was right with God and man and himself, he became the confident conqueror of the eighth chapter, watching from the hilltop of victory the surging battle at his feet; and in the peace that precedes victory, he exclaims, "We are more than conquerors."

If the social order is torn with confusion and noisy with tumult, it is because somewhere in the social order there is injustice and iniquity. If the mechanism of our civic and social life is grinding and grating upon the ears of our generation, it is because some foreign substance, some grit, something that should not be there has gotten into the running gear; and all the oils of philanthropy and all the unctuousness of our charity will not keep us from having our teeth set on edge. There must be social justice before there can be social peace; there must be social surgery before there can be social health.

Let us understand that in a certain sense there is something vastly more important than peace. There is nothing the devil desires more than to hear people singing about peace. For, let us realize, it is a false peace which makes the sin and the shame of our great cities possible. Indeed, it is a truth that there is nothing the devil and sin and darkness and crime and iniquity and political roguery desire so much as peace. At Jesus' birth the angels sang the world's peace anthem and his name is "the Prince of Peace," but it was Jesus himself who said, "I came not to send peace, but a sword"; and the last vision we catch of him before the record closes is this: "I saw heaven opened, and behold a white horse; and he that sat upon him was called Faithful and True, and in righteousness he doth judge and make war."

Wherever he goes, Jesus is the disturber of a false peace. Every one of his words is sharper than a two-edged sword. His gospel is like salt, and salt stings and burns before it purifies and heals. His truth is like leaven and leaven is a fermenting, agitating, exciting, ever-changing, transforming thing. His presence is like light, and before his coming evil things that grovel and hide in the darkness are revealed to their own undoing. His Church, sworn to preach peace, set the world in an uproar; and provoked its accusers to say, "These that have turned the world upside down are come hither also." Wherever there is anything wrong side up, it is the business of the Church to turn it wrong side down, whether it has its dwelling place in the cottage of the poor or the palace of the rich or the legislative halls of the nation. When Jesus came, "Herod the king . . . was troubled, and all Jerusalem with him." That is the way it is. When Jesus comes, the evil hides its face.

It is generally agreed among us that things today are not right, and until they are right there can be no permanent and enduring peace. It is not right for nations to hate each other. It is not right to glorify war. It is not right to say that national and individual morality have different standards of morals. It is not right for nations to break solemn pledges. It is not right to subjugate weak nations. It is not right to call weakness the sin against the Holy Spirit. It is not right to deify power, to rob the poor, to perpetuate poverty for political policies. Until things are right there can be no enduring peace. In the maps of the fifteenth century one can still see an undefined, unexplored, and mysterious section bearing the significant inscription, "*Hic sunt leones*" — "Here are the lions." There have been in the national policies of modern nations undefined, mysterious, suspicious sections of intrigue and diplomacy, over which we must write the words, "Here are the lions." Until the lions are discovered and slain there can be no assurance of security, no coming of the Prince of Peace.

At the heart of Christianity there is a cross, and that cross is a symbol of righteousness. Let us beware of evolving a religion that has no need for a cross. A religion without a cross, wherever it has appeared, has been both effeminate and inefficient. The cross in history and in Christian experience testifies to the moral character of God and his invincible righteousness.

If you will turn to the record, this is what you will read: "[He] made peace through the blood of his cross." "In Christ Jesus, ye who sometimes were far off are made nigh by the blood of Christ. For he is our peace, who hath made both one, and hath broken down the middle wall of partition . . . ; having abolished in his flesh the enmity, . . . so making peace." "For he hath made him to be sin for us, who knew no sin; that we might be made the righteousness of God in him." We cannot understand all that the cross means, and may never expect to understand it all, but we know that it is God's judgment on unrighteousness, that it is his sentence upon sin and his pledge of peace to a world that seeks shelter in the time of storm. We know that the Tree of Righteousness planted there on Calvary, deep-rooted in the eternal character of the all-holy God, still blossoms and bears the fruits of love, joy, and peace, throughout the world.

The earliest record of the Christian Church tells that the apostles were commissioned to go anywhere, "preaching peace by Jesus Christ," and then there is added the significant explanatory sentence, "He is Lord of all." We preach peace by Jesus Christ who is Lord of all.

Before we can live under the shelter of his peaceful reign, we must crown him Lord of all; and that is what men and nations refrain from doing. We have not yet put the government upon his shoulders. The fruit of righteousness is peace. We must crown him Lord of all. There is a song the children often sing, "Praise Him, praise Him, all ye little children." Sitting at the piano with a little lad one day, we were singing it together. It is one of those children's songs that run on through endless stanzas, satisfying and suggestive. We had sung it through as I thought: "Praise Him, praise Him, all ye little children"; "Love Him, love Him, all ye little children"; "Serve Him, serve Him, all ye little children." Then we stopped. The lad looked up, surprised and still expectant. "But we forgot to crown him," he said. And so we sang, "Crown Him, crown Him, all ye little children."

When we begin to think it through, we are confident that the little boy was right. We have forgotten to crown him. We have praised him with words of eloquent eulogy and with music of winsome melody. We have loved him, flattered him, sympathized with him, admired him, imitated him; but we have forgotten to crown him. We have forgotten that he is King. He is Lord of all. He is first of all King of Righteousness and after that, King of Peace.

25

The Only Way Out of the Dark

[BIBLE SUNDAY]

"*Thy word is a lamp unto my feet,*
And a light unto my path." — Ps. 119:105.

SOMETIME ago the American Bible Society published a pamphlet bearing the title *The Only Way Out of the Dark*. These seven words were printed in white on a perfectly black background. The blackness was apparent and curiosity was immediately aroused. When the four-page pamphlet was opened, all that was seen was the picture of a lovely Bible. The answer suggested, of course, was that the Bible is the only way out of the dark. It is the answer contained in the words, "Thy word is a lamp unto my feet, and a light unto my path."

The Word of God has indeed lighted the path of many a man lost in the darkness. It has lighted the way of thousands of pilgrims through the valley of the shadow of death. It has lighted nations down the course of their destiny and made them great. Mr. Stanley Baldwin, when he was prime minister of Great Britain, in speaking of the Bible called it "a high explosive." He said that the Bible contains great truths which unexpectedly stir the souls of men. One can never tell when the Bible will, as it were, blow up in one's face. Some flashing idea, struck from the truth of Scripture, might set men and nations on fire. Was it something along this line that Jesus had in mind when he said, "I am come to send fire upon the earth"?

It was a familiar saying of De Quincey that there are two types of literature. There are books of knowledge, books of science, encyclopedias, and dictionaries answering to the familiar slogan "Information, Please"; and then there are books of power, books that sway the spirits of men, books that deal with prophecy and poetry and imagination. Supreme among such books of this latter type is the Bible. For this reason Merezhkovski, the interpreter of the life of Jesus who wrote in Russian, once commented: "The world, as it now is, and the Book cannot continue together. Either the world must become other than it is, or the Book must disappear from the world."

We know what such a statement as that means and its implication might be applied to our own lives. No man and no nation can remain unchanged in the presence of an open Bible. Either the Bible remains a closed book or else you change your life. Can we say why that is so? Why has the Bible, containing the Word of God, such vitality, such potency, such explosive power?

For one thing, the Bible has its own way of writing history. In other words, the Bible is a *God-centered* book. When it is opened, we come immediately face to face with God. In the story of creation, which is sometimes criticized as being unscientific, the fact is at once made certain that behind the universe and behind all things that have been made there is God. In the very beginning, before light breaks across the face of the world, God is. When the world comes into being, we have the same word repeated over and over again: God. God saw; God made; God called; God created; God blessed; God finished his work. When we close the Book, we are again face to face with the vision of God, whom we see as the Eternal One, seated upon a throne guiding the destiny of men and nations.

In the second place, the Bible is *man-centered*. While the central reality and basic assurance of the Bible is God, nevertheless it is man in whom God is interested and for whom he gives his Son. When we think of those issues that divide the earth and separate the thinking of men, we are surprised to find how easily the Bible resolves the problem; for the Bible looks at life, not in terms of racial distinctions or national prestige, but in the larger aspect of humanity. Listen to its language: "He will judge the world in righteousness"; "This gospel . . . shall be preached in all the world"; "The kingdoms of this world are become the kingdoms of our Lord, and of his Christ"; "God so loved the world." In one of the prophets it is said of Pharaoh king of Egypt that he was "but a noise." Communism is but a noise, and so are all men and nations who have defied God and trampled upon the souls and bodies of other men. Follow through the pages of the Bible and you will find language and ideals that transcend anything that man is able to master even after the passing of the centuries. Listen to this: " In his days shall the righteous flourish; and abundance of peace so long as the moon endureth. He shall have dominion also from sea to sea, and from the river unto the ends of the earth. . . . For he shall deliver the needy when he crieth; the poor also, and him that hath no helper. . . . He shall redeem their soul from deceit and violence: and precious shall their blood be in his sight."

What a human book it is! We read of old men leaning on their staffs, little children crying in their cribs, mothers weeping over their dead, mothers laughing over their first-born, fathers worrying about their boys, brothers quarreling with each other, young men giving themselves to God. From page to page we read of all sorts of people moving across the stage of life — Jews and Greeks, Romans and Persians, Babylonians and Syrians, good men and bad men, wise men and fools, praying women and treacherous women, men loyal and heroic, little girls carrying news, little boys with their lunches, rich and poor, kings and slaves, black and white, strong and weak. Always there is the golden thread which ties the main content into a unity — tragedy and comedy, success and failure, life and death. And within it all God is always at the center. The earth is his footstool, the devil is in chains, and in every instance the conclusion reached is a true one.

Moses, for example, dies, but God's hand buries him. Elijah is beaten and driven and besieged, but he rides in the chariot of fire. Ruth, the alien, is crushed by death and sorrow, but in the end marries for love and we see her at last in her own home with her little baby boy. Job sits upon his ash heap covered with shame and failure, but in the end he is healed and all that he has lost is given back to him. Jonah is driven out into the sea and swallowed up by the whale, but in the last chapter peace and benediction reign. The prodigal son wanders off into the far country, but he comes back and there is singing and dancing when he returns. Jesus is crucified on a cross, but after three days he is let loose in the world, alive forevermore. No wonder, is it, that this is a book that sings and dances and rejoices with words that are set to the most majestic of the world's music?

The Bible deals not with little things but with big things. It deals not with dead issues but with living issues. It deals not with trivial things but with ultimate questions, questions that lie beneath all other questions: the questions science cannot answer; the questions politics cannot answer; the questions colleges cannot answer — questions like these: What is life? What is death? What is man? What is God? And at last, in the end, the answer comes. You will not perhaps find the final answer until you read on. Not until you go on do you hear the voice that says, "If it were not so, I would have told you." What is life? "This is life eternal, that they might know thee, the only true God." What is death? "Death is swallowed up in victory." What is man? "Now are we the sons of God." What is God? "God is a Spirit." "God is love."

The world as it now is and the Book cannot continue together. Either the world must change its ways or the Book will perish. They cannot both exist together. What will happen we know. We believe that not one promise of this Word will pass away until the dreams and hopes and prophecies contained in it shall be fulfilled and "the earth shall be full of the knowledge of the Lord, as the waters cover the sea."

26

"The Mountain Shall Be Thine"

[A BACCALAUREATE SERMON]

"But the mountain shall be thine; for it is a wood, and thou shalt cut it down: and the outgoings of it shall be thine: for thou shalt drive out the Canaanites, though they have iron chariots, and though they be strong." — Josh. 17:18.

THE land was at last occupied. The enemy had been driven back. The Israelites were in possession of their long-promised land. Joshua, the leader, was old but full of heroic ambition, and his first task on entering the country was to apportion the land to the twelve tribes according to their power and prestige. Soon the various tribes had taken up the territory assigned to them. They were all satisfied except the powerful tribe of Joseph, whose territory was in the very center of the land stretching from the Jordan to the Mediterranean. It included the Plain of Sharon and some of the finest and most productive land in the whole of Palestine. Nevertheless Ephraim and Manasseh, which made up the tribe of Joseph, were dissatisfied, and because Joshua belonged to their tribe, they made their complaint more readily, thinking it would be easy for him to grant them further favor. "Why hast thou given . . . [us] but one lot," they asked, "and one portion to inherit, seeing . . . [we are] a great people?"

We no sooner read these words and hear this complaint than we feel that it has a modern touch to it. It is the very thing that is happening today. People are still dissatisfied with their inheritance. They complain that it is too small, their allotment too meager, their rights overlooked, and they feel as those who have been dispossessed. Perhaps there is ground for complaint and there is reason why the rumblings of discontent are heard. Why should it be thought something strange for young women and shop girls, men in mines and factories, to complain of their unequal share of inheritance? One is born to the inheritance of health and happiness, another to the handicap of poverty and physical frailty, and life seems to pile up its account against the poor.

What did Joshua say to this complaining tribe? The record is very interesting. The old hero replied — and there is just the suggestion of a sting in his words: "If thou be a great people, then get thee up to the wood country, and cut down for thyself there in the land of the Perizzites and of the giants, if mount Ephraim be too narrow for thee." Go up to the high places, said Joshua, and every foot of land that you capture and secure shall be yours. The people, however, demurred, saying, "The hill is not enough for us: and all the Canaanites that dwell in the land of the valley have chariots of iron, both they who are in Beth-shean and her towns, and they who are of the valley of Jezreel." Again Joshua replied — and there is a suggestion of subtle irony repeated in his words: "Thou art a great people, and hast great power: thou shalt not have one lot only: but the mountain shall be thine; for it is a wood, and thou shalt cut it down: and the outgoings of it shall be thine: for thou shalt drive out the Canaanites, though they have iron chariots, and though they be strong."

This was the answer of a man who knew what it was to fight for his own inheritance. "Go and win your inheritance," he said. Use your skill and your brains and your courage. Because some may have a greater share is no reason why you have less. The land is not all occupied. The places are not yet all filled. The wealth has not yet all been gathered in. Because one man lives in luxury is not the reason others live in poverty. There is glory and goods enough for all in this land of plenty. It is only a fool's view to say that because one man is up, another man is down. The wealth of the world is not in one pot or in one bank or in one family or in one nation.

Such is the implication that lies behind the reasoning of this Old Testament warrior. There are economic lies just as there are moral lies, and it is an economic lie to say that there is just so much wealth and that if you get more than your share I, therefore, must get less. The distribution of wealth cannot be achieved on that basis. For the assumption is not valid. Wealth does not consist of gold that is in the bank, or of money that is in your pocket. Wealth is in the ground, in the air, in the rivers, in the forests, in the orchards, in the mills and factories, in your brain; and from these factories, forests, farms, mills, and mines wealth is constantly increasing and enlarging and multiplying. We are wealthier today than we were yesterday, and we shall be still wealthier tomorrow. The secret of having and possessing is not in cutting and dividing and sharing what we now possess, but in creating, developing, and discovering the new wealth which is ready to be uncovered. Verily, the mountain shall be yours. There is much land still to be possessed and there is wealth to be created. We shall get on best by exploring new territory, new worlds, instead of quarreling over the wealth already created.

In the little laboratory where Thomas Edison worked out his first experiments, it is interesting and entrancing to see the crude mechanism by which he felt his way to the incandescent light and to the revolving disks from which he heard his own voice coming back to himself. What a mountain he had climbed! What new territories he had explored! What new wealth he had uncovered! And if he were here today, a young man beginning life again, he would begin where he left off by exploring still new countries, by discovering other new mountains, by uncovering greater new wealth.

There are other men, and women too, who, like Edison, have begun life with empty hands and empty pockets and who toiled to win for themselves and others the place that they now occupy. The joy of that struggle is their finest memory. The days of struggle and sacrifice are good days. The days of paternalism are never good days. The days for having things done for us are not the creative days. The days when citizens are provided with crutches are not healthy days, and we need to hear today the recall of Joshua to valor and heroism, when the spirit moves men to glorious living. We need to hear the voice that Kipling refers to, the voice that he says is as sure as conscience, ringing the interminable changes on the everlasting whisper, day and night, repeated so:

> " 'Something hidden. Go and find it. Go
> and look behind the Ranges—
> Something lost behind the Ranges.
> Lost and waiting for you. Go!' "
> —*From "The Explorer."*

This is why there can be no truce between Christianity and Communism. The end of Communism is to attain worldly goods, and there are no other goods for the Communist. And to get worldly goods they must be seized; they must be taken from those who already have them. The motive of Communism is class hatred, violence, war, anything, in fact, to enable those who have not to seize upon the goods of those who have. Christianity, on the other hand, impels us not to take but to give, not to seize but to share, not to hate but to love, not to destroy men's lives but to save them. It calls upon men everywhere to live creatively and labor in the vineyard of the Lord. Between Communism and Christianity there is a gulf fixed, and it is impossible for anyone to be on both sides of that divided gulf.

Furthermore, this same principle gives us the assurance that Christianity can never be a complacent religion. The same principle that operates in the natural world obtains in the spiritual world. The world of the spirit is inexhaustible. There are vast unexplored areas to be opened up in the realm of Christian living. We are not the Christians that we ought to be. There are new territories still to be occupied in the world of Christian fellowship. There are new roads to be broken in the way of Christian benevolence. As Christians, we have not yet learned to give as we ought to give. There is not just so much wealth to be distributed through the churches. There are vast untapped resources awaiting the service of God and man. There are high mountains yet to be scaled in Christian sacrifice. I hear the voice of the prophet out of the past: "O Zion, that bringest good tidings, get thee up into the high mountain; O Jerusalem, that bringest good tidings, lift up thy voice with strength; lift it up, be not afraid; say unto the cities of Judah, Behold your God!"

Sunday by Sunday, as I look into the faces of the men and women who come to worship and realize the positions they occupy in their businesses and professions, I know what God could do through them for the spiritual and temporal betterment of this land. The prophet is right. If we lift up our eyes, we can behold God standing ready, armed to serve and to lead. "Behold your God!" What he could do for us! It is as if Michelangelo were standing outside a house, looking in through the window, seeing the easel, the brushes, the paint, everything ready and waiting for the master, and saying to himself, "If I were inside, what a picture I could paint!" Say to the churches of America, "Behold your God!" He is ready. "Behold, I stand at the door, and knock." What a life he could make! What a Church he could create!

The book of The Acts, in telling the story of the Early Church, says, "Great fear fell upon the people." That is the New Testament way of speaking of the presence of the supernatural. A Church that is not made quiet and reverent and expectant by the unquestioned presence of God will never be a power in the world. "Get thee up into the high mountain." Say to the people of America, "Behold your God!"

27

Christ – the Hope of the World

"*And he is before all things, and by him all things consist.*" — Col. 1:17.

IN one of the war-ruined churches in Flanders, which exploding shells had all but destroyed, there could be seen upon the side of a broken wall a Scripture motto. It stood out against the fierce destruction that had ruined altar and organ, chancel and tower. It was this text in Latin: "*Instaurare Omnia in Christo.*" Our English Bible translates the text, "By him all things consist." The Revised Version comes closer to it: "In him all things consist." Moffatt comes still closer to it: "He is prior to all, and all coheres in him." Weymouth is still nearer: "He is before all things, and in and through Him the universe is one harmonious whole."

Saint Paul championed the thesis that all things hold together in Christ. That potent Scriptural motto, clinging to the fragment of broken wall in the ruined church in Flanders, challenges the world at its worst. Everything was burning up — treaties and covenants, towns and homes, churches and civilization itself; but as we now look back, Christ alone went through that furnace of fire and came out with undiminished glory. Everything else suffered. All our vaunted progress, our science, our smug ideas of religion — all had the touch of fire upon them. He alone walked in the midst of the fire and upon him the touch of the fire had no power.

This, then, is our theme. Christ is the only hope of world unity. Only by him and around him and in him can we find our dreams and hopes fulfilled.

Let us think, first, in terms of international relationships — an area that occupies much of our thinking today. The world has become a trading community. We cannot avoid entangling alliances. Isolation is impossible. There was a day when China could keep the world from entering her domain. She built a great wall around her northern boundary. She closed her seaports. She built high walls around her cities. She shut herself in and all others out and claimed for herself immunity from foreign influence. That day is done. Those very walls have been rebuilt into highways over which the commerce of the world can travel.

No nation can separate itself by stone walls or tariff walls from other nations. Isolation is impossible. A prominent financier has given it as his opinion that no man should think that "the living standards of America can be permanently maintained at a measurably higher level than those of the other civilized countries. Either we shall lift theirs to ours or they will drag ours down to theirs." But around what standard shall we gather in order to lift the productive capacity and consuming power to a point equal to our own? Whose name will be on our lips as we seek to secure a more peaceable world? The old names are gone forever. There are, however, new names potent enough to stir a whole nation. There are the names of Lenin and Stalin. There is the name of Nehru or Chiang Kai-shek. These are names having an international value, but not one of them is capable of binding the world into a unity of purpose.

Only one name has international significance today, and across the barriers of race and religion His name binds the nations in a golden hope. If put to the final test, what is it that the people of the world say they want? They say, "We want what Christ has to give." What is it that we say we are seeking for? We seek what Christ has already found. What is it that we want? We want peace and love and contentment and blessing. We need Christ. That is the answer we would give. It is the answer Sir Philip Gibbs gave in the closing analysis of the war years. "My own belief," he said, "is that the war was no proof against the Christian faith, but rather a revelation that we are desperately in need of the Spirit of Christ."

Let us look at our own land. Where do we find in America a bond that will bind the different peoples of our nation in unity?

Crime continues; lawlessness increases; political issues arise; but the citizenship is indifferent. Everywhere the atmosphere is one of unconcern and apathy. It is only when moral values are touched and the religious note is heard that men and women rise up to enter the arena to do battle for their convictions. If it is true that political issues fail to arouse the people, it is because the moral and spiritual note is missing from the appeal of our leaders. However, whenever that note is struck, there is immediate response.

In a memorable address made some years ago, which was entitled "America Is Too Rich to Be Loved," Mr. Owen D. Young remarked on the fact that "after all we must remember that politics and economics are not the masters of men — they are their servants." If we sense the necessity for spiritual development, for service, for humility, for friendliness, for a higher helpfulness, where shall we look to find these things? They will be found wherever the Spirit of Christ is found. For in him cohere all the values of life that unify men's hearts in a passionate devotion.

Let us look at another aspect of this same problem, our social order, which is one of the finest in the world but is far from being a unity. There is a great gulf dividing sections of our people. There are the rich and the poor, the privileged and the underprivileged, the strong and the weak, the dominant and the recessive. Where shall we find the bridge to throw across these separating gulfs? How shall we close the chasms and bring in the Kingdom of God, the brotherhood of man? It is only the Spirit of Christ that can accomplish it. Only as we see through his eyes, do we see the infinite value of every single human life. The norm of Christian ethics lies in this, that every human being is of value in the sight of God.

Everywhere where the spirit of Christ comes, human life takes on new value. Where the name of Christ is unknown, life is incomparably cheap. Jesus looked out upon the multitude, divided by more impossible gulfs than any that exist in our social order today, and saw not a mob but the family of God; and he spoke to them of their Father, who claimed them all as his children and yearned over them with a love that was broader and wider and deeper than the measure of man's mind.

Furthermore, let us say that all the rivalries, divisions, animosities, and separations that we discover in society and in the world are but a portion of the rivalries, the divisions, the separations, that are discovered in the life of each of us. Only when we are unified and redeemed personally shall we have a unified and redeemed social order. We are what the psychologists call "split personalities." We take sides against ourselves. The things that we want to do we do not and the things that we do not want to do, we do. It is as Paul said, "The good that I would, I do not; but the evil which I would not, that I do." We are a divided self, a double personality, a soul that is in the grip of contending forces.

That is why Christ demands what he calls a new birth, in which the old personality is reborn, redeemed, and unified. From the human point of view, conversion is the unification of life. You cannot unify the human heart around anything that is human. Such human centers are too small, too trivial, too circumscribed. The human heart is made for God, and only in him will the instincts and aspirations of life be satisfied.

Robert Browning has a wonderful picture of how Christ captivates and conquers and unifies all of life. "Not even Christ Himself can save man else than as He holds man's soul; and therefore did He come into our flesh As some wise hunter creeping on his knees With a torch, into the blackness of some cave, To face and quell the beast there, — take the soul, And so possess the whole man, body and soul." What a picture it is! Christ, coming like a hunter into a dark cave as some wild beast crouches ready to spring, slays the beast and carries into freedom the soul that has been in the grip of the evil thing; and so sets free the whole man — body and soul. When Christ takes up his abode in our hearts, all lesser loyalties yield to him and in him all things find their rightful place.

Section Six

THE CHRISTIAN CHURCH

28

The Church

"There is one body, and one Spirit, even as ye are called in one hope of your calling." — Eph. 4:4.

It is an arresting and challenging thought that in the creed of the Christian Church belief in the Church takes its place beside belief in God. It is high company the Church keeps. "I believe in the holy Catholic Church; the communion of saints; the forgiveness of sins; the resurrection of the body; and the life everlasting." This is the position of the Church not only in the Apostles' Creed but in all the Catholic creeds. The Nicene Creed, the most authoritative of all the Catholic creeds, after expressing belief in "the Holy Ghost; the Lord and Giver of Life," continues with the words, "And I believe one Holy Catholic and Apostolic Church." The Church holds the same place in our liturgies and hymnals. Down through the years we have been singing, "The Church's one Foundation is Jesus Christ her Lord," "I love Thy Church, O God," "Glorious things of thee are spoken, Zion, City of our God." The New Testament itself holds the high view of the Church. We have such expressions as these: "I speak," says Saint Paul, "concerning Christ and the church"; and asserts, "Christ also loved the church, and gave himself for it." We read of "the church of the living God, the pillar and ground of the truth." In receiving the confession of Peter, Jesus himself said, "Upon this rock I will build my church; and the gates of hell shall not prevail against it."

This high view is in contrast to much of the thought of our age. We have been critical of the Church. The question is repeatedly asked, What is wrong with the Church? Contrary to the fact, it seems to be the consensus that the Church is not having the success it ought to have. Its back is to the wall. Of course, this has always been true, for Christianity has always had to fight for its life. If we knew history better, we should realize that there have been darker periods in the life of the Church than we have ever experienced. It has again and again been all but driven from the field. Explanations that do not explain have been given for this situation.

There are those who are out of sorts with the Church's creed, its ecclesiasticism, its dogmatism, its missionary policy. They pass harsh judgments. Many of these men and women are among our best citizens. They support the forward-looking social programs of their community. They are eager for political and educational reform. They are on the side of the upward swing of society. They are honest and sincere, and intellectual integrity is their one desire.

And there are also other critics who are even more severe in their charges. They are secularists rather than pagans; for paganism, at least, did possess religious passion. Such people reply to all invitations to identify themselves with the Church that they see no need. They get along very well without it, they say. They do not need to pray. If they are in need, they ask themselves or the Government. To them the Church is irrelevant, superfluous. There is some advantage to this outspoken indifference. It is morally honest. It saves the Church from fighting shadows. There is little use of people going to church who do not want to go, and no social stigma rests upon those who set the Church to one side. However, it must be said that there is something wrong with people whose religious sense has atrophied. The straight thinking of the saints cannot be ignored. The Bible states that "the world," as we know it, "lieth in wickedness." The tragic sense of life is a fact. Sin is a reality, and men in all ages have exchanged the truth of God for a lie.

There are people who are out of sympathy with the things the Church stands for. The Church stands for a certain definite interpretation of life, of death, of the world; and there are people who do not like that interpretation. The Church stands for the interpretation of life in terms of the cross, of death in terms of judgment, of the world in terms of Fatherhood of God, who is over all and in all. It stands for a definite revelation of God in history, and men and women who have assimilated a theory of inevitable evolution cannot be in sympathy with God's making his approach to the world at a definite date in time.

In the New Testament the Church is spoken of under three different figures. Sometimes it is referred to as a building, sometimes as the body of Christ, and sometimes as the bride of Christ. Let us see if we cannot gather under these easily understood figures of speech the essential things that should be said in any interpretation of the holy Catholic Church, in which our faith rests.

The Church is like a building. It was the symbol our Lord used in his great word to his disciples, "Upon this rock I will build my church." It suggests security, stability, permanency. And it is interesting to notice how Jesus speaks of the Church as "my church." Apart from him there is no Church. We can neither create nor destroy a Church. It is not our Church. We cannot do with it what we like. We cannot say in it what we choose. We cannot use it for our own ends. It is Christ's Church. He is its builder and maker. It is his message that the Church proclaims. It is his salvation that the Church offers. It is in his presence that the Church rejoices. It is Christ's people who alone constitute the Church.

The Church is nothing apart from the Christian folk who in Christ are built up into a spiritual fellowship. Money and brains, authority and organization, ritual and philanthropy cannot make a Church. An orator cannot make a Church: he can make an audience. An audience is like a heap of stones, but a Church is a spiritual building.

Because it is Christ's Church, it has stability and permanency. "The gates of hell shall not prevail against it." Churches rise and pass away, but the Church abides. The Christian Church has only one asset, one message. It cannot rival the world. The world can rival and outclass the Church on almost every issue but one. It can outclass our preaching. The world can give better music, better architecture, a more appealing ritual, finer organization, a more immediate social program. There is only one direction in which the Church can go. The gate is strait and the way is narrow. The only asset the Church has is Christ.

The Church is the body of Christ. It is not an organization. It is an organism. The word "ecclesia" signifies that people are "called out" of one social order into another. They are called out of the world into the family of God, into the household of faith; and in this new society there is life and unity. The body is alive, and this mark of the Christian Church is emphasized again and again.

It is this Church, made up of the redeemed family of God, that is one and catholic. Ignatius long ago said, "Where Jesus is, there is the Catholic Church." The word "catholic" means universal. There can be only one Church. The Church of Christ is one because the same life pulsates through the entire body. This is the true way to think of catholicity — as a spirit that binds the churches of Christendom in a bond stronger than time, stronger than death. The truth that unites is stronger and more enduring than that which separates and divides; and the true argument for union is not derived from good feeling or economy in finance but from the compelling conviction that we make manifest to the world what we know to be a fact, that the Church is one in Jesus Christ.

The attractive power of such a Church will soon be evident, and this can be done only where Christ is the unifying center, the Object of our adoration. When the Christian community achieves this end, it will not fear the encroachments of Communism or the challenge of a secular nationalism. In a volume of sermons by an evangelical Scot, the truth is thus plainly set forth: "To save men; to save society; to banish disease and sin; to dethrone vice and selfishness; to overthrow the kingdom of Satan and bring in the realm of God; to mediate the riches of God's salvation to a perishing world; to make the kingdoms of the world the Kingdom of God and of his Christ — these are the things that supremely matter. If the Church were a redemptive fellowship of men and women, bound together to achieve these ends, to express the mind and will of Christ alone, to make his purpose of world regeneration effective and all-prevailing, then all lovers of good life would really be in her fellowship. At least the last shred of excuse for holding back would be torn from the Church's detractors. If there be any reality and substance in the reasons usually put forward by this class for refusal to shoulder the Church's burden, then a revitalized Church with Christ's Spirit and purpose glowing at the heart of it would compel such men's respect and allegiance. Such a Church could no longer be judged by them. She herself would be their judge."

The Church is the bride of Christ. This mystical language suggests a personal union that is spiritual and vital. The idea symbolized in this figure is, of course, that of attractive loveliness. There is a book bearing the name *The Heritage of Beauty*, which contains photographs of Christian churches in all lands, especially in foreign lands where Christianity has been introduced during the immediate past. It shows great cathedrals and humble chapels built after the architecture of the lands where they have been erected — Japan, China, India, Syria, Africa. It is an attractive study. But architecture, however beautiful, is not the "glory" of the Church. The true glory of the Church consists in the lives of redeemed men and women who in Christ have been transfigured.

The Christian Church is thus a fellowship, a society of Christian people who seek to serve God. No man can do his best work alone. He needs other men to think with him and work with him. We join hands with those who have the same purpose. We join hands with Baptists and Methodists and Episcopalians and Presbyterians and Quakers and all who love Christ and seek to serve him. Because there are people who believe in God the Father Almighty, and in Jesus Christ his Son our Lord, and in the Holy Spirit, there is of necessity a Church.

29

The Gospel

"Now after that John was put in prison, Jesus came into Galilee, preaching the gospel of the kingdom of God." — Mark 1:14.

THE religion of Christianity is called the gospel. It is the only religion that is rightly so described. It is the one word to which the New Testament returns time and again. "Jesus went about preaching the gospel of the kingdom." Saint Mark begins his story of Jesus with the words, "The beginning of the gospel of Jesus Christ." Saint Paul states that his mission in the world was to "testify the gospel of the grace of God." In the imperial city of Rome he announced that he was "not ashamed of the gospel of Christ."

The attempt has been made to adopt the word and to apply it to other messages and other programs. Books are written bearing the titles "The Gospel of Wealth," "The Gospel of Labor," "The Gospel of Communism," "The Gospel of Disarmament," "The Gospel of Peace"; but all these are particular and partial points of view. We could say even today, as Saint Paul said long ago, "Though we, or an angel from heaven, preach any other gospel unto you . . . , let him be accursed." All of which means that there is and can be only one gospel, the glorious gospel of the grace of God which has been revealed in Jesus Christ. Concerning the gospel, there are three things at least to be said.

First, the gospel is not good advice: it is good news. It contains much good advice, but that is not primarily its message. The Sermon on the Mount, the teachings of Jesus, the reiterated counsels of Saint Paul, all contain memorable advice that has passed into proverbs. The New Testament contains advice concerning home and family life, concerning good will and race relations, concerning temperance and self-control, concerning love and the kindness to be shown to enemies. The New Testament is the best treatise on good advice that there is, but the gospel itself is more than good advice: it is good news. It is the announcement of a fact that has altered life at its center. It is the good news concerning the revelation of God in the person of Jesus Christ. Consequently, the preacher of the gospel is a herald of a message and not a dispenser of advice. The preacher who is satisfied to give out good advice and neglect the heralding of the good news has missed his calling. We may be interested in what this or that doctor of divinity thinks about this or that, but it is not particularly important what he personally thinks. What we want to know from him is concerning what he has heard and knows about the good news that has come to us from the unseen world.

Secondly, the gospel is not good news about the world, but good news about God. We can find out about the world from other sources. The newspapers and the magazines and the radio will tell us about the world. If we accept what they tell us, it is a world of racial hatred and class cruelty. It is a world of misery and weariness, of sorrow and pain. It is a world that can do nothing with some folks but restrain them from evil, shutting them up in prisons and penitentiaries. It is a world of sunshine and shadows, a world that sends one woman singing on her way and silences the song in the hearts of others.

Science too will tell us about the world. If we accept the story that science tells, then we shall believe that the world is burning itself out, that the stars are cooling, and that in the far future our earth will belong in the cemetery of dead worlds. The gospel is not good news about the world: it is good news about God; and being good news about God, it issues in good news for all mankind.

Also, there is good news in the New Testament about the social order. But we shall find the same good news elsewhere. We shall find the outline of an ideal social order in textbooks on socialism and Communism and political science. We shall find a new social order set forth in a score of current magazines and on a hundred lecture platforms. We shall find it set forth in the Prophets of the Old Testament, and if it is only the program of a social order we need, we may do away with our New Testament and the teaching of Jesus and cling to Isaiah and Micah and Amos and Jonah, the first among the internationalists.

Where shall we find the glowing hope of a social order more luminous than we find it in the familiar words, penned centuries before the coming of Christ: "In the last days it shall come to pass, that the mountain of the house of the Lord shall be established in the top of the mountains, and it shall be exalted above the hills; and people shall flow unto it. And many nations shall come, and say, Come, and let us go up to the mountain of the Lord, and to the house of the God of Jacob; and he will teach us of his ways, and we will walk in his paths: for the law shall go forth of Zion, and the word of the Lord from Jerusalem. And he shall judge among many people, and rebuke strong nations afar off; and they shall beat their swords into plowshares, and their spears into pruning hooks: nation shall not lift up a sword against nation, neither shall they learn war any more. But they shall sit every man under his vine and under his fig tree; and none shall make them afraid: for the mouth of the Lord of hosts hath spoken it."

Jesus was interested in this new social order and he began his ministry by identifying himself with it. His first sermon was preached from the text taken from the prophet Isaiah, "The Spirit of the Lord is upon me, because he hath anointed me to preach the gospel to the poor; he hath sent me . . . to preach deliverance to the captives, and recovering of sight to the blind, to set at liberty them that are bruised, to preach the acceptable year of the Lord."

Jesus, however, did not champion any form of social order. If he had done so, he would long since have ceased to be our Master and our Saviour. He has set before us no social pattern to be copied. We cannot even speak accurately of a Christian social order, as if Jesus had authorized some social standard or some form of civilization to which we can attain.

The good news about the Kingdom of God, which Jesus proclaimed, is that it is a Kingdom of "righteousness, and peace, and joy in the Holy Ghost." The Kingdom of God does not come out of a social order; the social order comes out of the Kingdom of God. The Kingdom of God comes not from anything men can see or will see regarding political or economic or social organization; for, lo, " the kingdom of God is within you, " said Jesus.

It was George Tyrrell who once remarked, " When everyone has been adequately fed, clothed, sheltered, the question still remains what to do with life." We might go on to ask, after war has been forever outlawed and all racial bitterness changed to good will and the industrial order redeemed, what will we do with life and where will our restless hearts find rest? That is the central question with which the gospel deals. " Behold, I make all things new " — that is the message of the gospel, and it begins by making new hearts, new lives, new men; and without new men we cannot have any new order. The gospel begins by preaching the doctrine of the new birth. " Except a man be born again, he cannot see the kingdom of God."

One other word needs to be said. The Gospel is good news about the life that lies beyond this life. It opens the door into the land that lies beyond death. It lights the dark country which lies beyond our sight but not beyond our dreams. It says to us that now we are the children of God. It crowns life with immortality. A soldier, blinded in the war, had his sight restored by a delicate operation. When he saw the light, he said: " When the bandage fell from my eyes, I walked into a new world of hope, faith, and beauty. This world is in my heart and I will walk in it till I die." So do we feel when the gospel of gladness takes hold of us.

30

What Protestant Christians Believe

[REFORMATION SUNDAY]

"*Knowing that a man is not justified by the works of the law, but by the faith of Jesus Christ, even we have believed in Jesus Christ, that we might be justified by the faith of Christ, and not by the works of the law: for by the works of the law shall no flesh be justified.*" — Gal. 2:16.

THE big word in our religion is the word "Christian." The big question is not what Protestants believe, but what Christians believe. And the big question is easy to answer. Chrstians believe in Jesus Christ as their Saviour and Lord, and seek to follow him in all things. But Christianity as a religion has expressed itself in creeds, in institutions, in church life and work, and has become quite a complex affair. As a result of a long history, Christianity has expressed itself in what may be called distinct patterns. While these patterns have much in common, they are nevertheless different expressions or interpretations of the Christian faith.

There is (1) the Protestant pattern, which claims that in all questions of doctrine and of life the Bible is the final authority. Protestants appeal to the Bible in all discussions and disputes regarding conduct or creed or church. There is (2) the Roman pattern, known as the Roman Catholic Church, which is governed by a hierarchy, the supreme authority being the pope of Rome, which claims authority over the souls of men. There is (3) the Greek Catholic pattern, known officially as The Holy Orthodox Catholic Apostolic Eastern Church, including in its area of special influence Greece, Russia, the Balkan States, and the Near East. It too claims exclusive authority and refuses to recognize the claims of Protestant or Roman Churches.

These three Churches — the Protestant; the Roman, or Western; the Greek, or Eastern — profess the faith set forth in the general creeds of Christendom, such as the Apostles' Creed and the Nicene Creed. They each claim to be catholic, that is, universal; and all alike believe:

> In God the Father, Maker of heaven and earth;
> In Jesus Christ, His only Son, our Lord;
> In the Holy Ghost, the Lord and Giver of Life;
> In the holy Catholic Church;
> In the communion of saints;
> In the forgiveness of sins;
> In the life everlasting.

These truths are the common possession of all Christians, and no one Church has exclusive claim upon them. These fundamental teachings of the Christian faith Protestants believe, and seek to translate them into character and conduct.

History

It has often been pointed out that all religions have a tendency to drift from their early loyalties. Like a river that absorbs something of the soil through which it flows, so a religion assimilates to itself customs and practices of the area or historical period where it has taken root. This is true of such religions as Buddhism, Hinduism, Mohammedanism, and it is also true of Christianity. Our soldiers and sailors who have been in many places have seen the same religion differently expressed in far separated lands. The Christianity of the Middle Ages, in both the Roman and the Greek Churches, was different from the early Christianity and from the Christianity of today. There were certain practices and customs incorporated into the Church that had no New Testament authority and were disturbing to many devout Christians in the sixteenth century, when the religious revival, known as the Reformation, shook the Church in the West to its foundation. No such revival took place in the Eastern Church, but the revival within the Western Church created what is now known as Protestantism.

The name "Protestant" implies that the churches of the Reformation, led by men like Martin Luther and John Calvin, "protested" against customs and practices of the Church that were contrary to the teaching of the New Testament. They demanded a return to the simplicity and purity of early Christianity. They themselves were Roman Catholics, appealing for revival and reform within their own Church, and when this was denied, they formed themselves into Christian fellowships or churches, calling themselves "Evangelicals" and later "Protestants." While the name "Protestant" came into use at the time of the Reformation in the sixteenth century, the Protestant position proclaimed was not new, but was a definite return to the simplicity of the Christian gospel as set forth in the New Testament. The Reformation was not a detour from the main highway, but a return to the highway. It was an act of loyalty to the gospel on the part of representatives of the then existing Church, who were convinced that the Church of that day had departed from the truth made known in the Christian revelation.

Let this fact, then, be clear: Protestantism is no recently created religion, but is the continuation of true apostolic Christianity. It did not begin with Luther or Calvin. It began with the gospel. It began with the life and death and resurrection of Christ. It began when the Early Church began, and when the Church departed from the simplicity of early Christianity this revival re-established the simplicity and centrality of the gospel. When, therefore, the question is asked, "What do Protestants believe?" the answer is made, "Protestants believe what the New Testament and the Early Church teach and proclaim."

The Bible

Protestants believe in the Bible. They make their appeal not to the Church — not to a priest, bishop, pope, or patriarch — but to the word of God found in the Scriptures of the Old and New Testaments, the only infallible rule of faith and life. Protestants believe that the Bible needs no other interpreter than the Holy Spirit. They believe, however, in the best scholarship as an aid to the interpretation of the Scriptures. They have labored earnestly to put the Bible into the hands of the people in their own language. Believing that Bible study is necessary to Christian living, they have sought everywhere to teach people to read the Bible for themselves. The first task of Protestant missionaries has been to give the people the Bible in their own language and to teach them to read it. Protestants, therefore, have been pioneers in Bible translation and have organized and supported the great world-encircling Bible societies. This is a fact worth thinking about. No prayer book — valuable as it may be — no symbolism of the cross, no crucifix, no formal recitation of a creed, no authority of church or council, can take the place of the Bible. The Bible, read under the guidance of the Holy Spirit, is the Christian's authoritative guide. Protestants therefore claim that they truly represent and interpret Christianity as it is set forth in the Bible. They hold that anyone who will read the Bible prayerfully, with the aid of the best scholarship, will reach the conclusion that Protestantism honestly interprets the teachings and conforms to the practices of early Christianity.

The Gospel

Protestants believe in the gospel. The gospel is good news. It is good news about God. It is good news about man. It is good news about sin. It is good news about life. It is good news about death.

The good news about God is that he is our Father, which is Jesus' favorite name for God. The good news about man is that he is a child of God, made in the image of God, free and immortal. The good news about sin is that sin can be forgiven. "If we confess our sins, he [God] is faithful and just to forgive us our sins, and to cleanse us from all unrighteousness." That is direct action. God's forgiveness is full and free, and is not conditioned on good works, or merit, or penance, or the prayers of saints, or the words of preacher or priest. It is God's good gift to men, for forgiveness means, not the avoidance of penalty, but restoration to favor. It is God who saves. It is Christ who died for us. No man can save himself. The Church cannot save him. The sacraments cannot save him. God alone can save.

The Church

Protestants believe in the Church. They believe that the Church was founded by Jesus Christ himself. He is the head of the Church. The Church is his body. The Church is not primarily an organization or an institution, but a society of believers, a brotherhood, a fellowship of the faithful. The Church is the people of God. Where Christians are gathered together in the name of Christ, there is the Church. Protestants believe that every man has direct access to God through Christ. They believe in the "priesthood of believers," holding that every Christian has immediate, direct, personal, and effective approach to God through Christ. Christ is still present in his Church. The Church is his body. This does not mean that Protestants do not hold in high esteem pastors and priests who have been ordained to the gospel ministry, but it does mean that wherever the Gospel is truly preached and the sacraments truly administered there is the Christian Church.

The State

Protestants believe in democracy. Protestant countries tend to be democratic countries. Fascism does not flourish in such Protestant soil as that of the United States, Great Britain, Canada, Australia, Holland, Norway. In Germany freedom of worship was denied in order that Fascism might succeed. Protestants believe in freedom. Their influence helped to write freedom into the Declaration of Independence. They believe in a free Church that will not tolerate dictation by the State. They believe in a free State that will not tolerate dictation by the Church. They believe in democracy because they believe that God alone is Lord of man's conscience. They believe in democracy because God has endowed man with certain inalienable rights such as life, liberty, and the pursuit of happiness. No State can take these rights away, and no Church nullify them. They are God-given and inalienable. It is this faith that demands for all men everywhere open books, open schools, open courts, open churches, open assemblies. If you are a Protestant, the liberty you claim for yourself must be extended also to all other men. If you are a Protestant, no State, no Church, no party, can control your voice or your vote. If you are a Protestant, you must be tolerant of all other sincere types of religious experience and you must not deny to others that same freedom of worship which you claim for yourself. If you are a Protestant, you cannot transfer your responsibility for your salvation to any individual or any Church. You must make your own choice. You cannot surrender your soul to anyone but to the Lord Jesus Christ. You must swear allegiance to him and to him only. Beneath the denominational differences, which belong to Protestantism and which are frequently mentioned to its discredit, there is an inner spiritual unity not born of compulsion or constraint but rooted in an unanswering loyalty to the Christ who is both Saviour and Lord. To believe in him, to love him, to follow him, to serve him — this is the Christian creed and this is the Protestant faith. Protestantism exalts the greatest word ever spoken to men: "God so loved the world, . . . that whosoever believeth in him should not perish, but have everlasting life."

31

What Memorial Have You?

[STEWARDSHIP SUNDAY]

"*Verily I say unto you, Wheresoever this gospel shall be preached throughout the whole world, this also that she hath done shall be spoken of for a memorial of her.*" — Mark 14:9.

It is easy to give away other people's money. It is such a pleasant and painless experience that we catch ourselves frequently indulging in it. The larger the sum of money that is given away, the better we like spending it. When we read the wills of men and women who distribute their wealth, we are sure that we could have disposed of their estate in a far better way. We are sure we can handle other people's money better than they do themselves. We are expert in the distribution of someone else's beneficence.

There is a striking example of this very thing in the life of Jesus. He had come to Bethany, where Lazarus had been raised from the dead, on the last Sabbath of his life. He had come there in high courage, notwithstanding the fact that a price had been put upon his head. We are not told how he spent the Sabbath, but when the evening came, a feast was prepared for him, and his devoted friends were the guests. The feast was spread in the home of Simon, who had been a leper, and Mary and Martha were there. As usual, Martha was serving, and, as usual Lazarus was silent. It was Mary who gained the center of interest. Quietly and unnoticed, she slipped away and procured a jar of precious ointment. The Bible does not say much in praise of money, but in each of the Gospel records it is stated that Mary's ointment was very precious, very costly. It was estimated as worth three hundred pence, and when you remember that a penny was a day's wage, then the worth of the ointment will be valued at a year's wages for a man. This precious perfume, extracted from a rare plant in Arabia, was contained in an alabaster jar, fragile and transparent as light. Mary took it, crushed the jar, and poured out the ointment upon the head and hair and feet of Jesus. It was a ceremony that belonged only to royalty, and was such as only a monarch could expect to receive. And — the record is quite explicit — she poured it all out. A few drops might have sufficed, but she gave it all. She let it all flow out, and the exquisite fragrance of it filled the whole house.

It was a gift that only wealth could give, and it awakened among the guests violent reactions. Matthew in his Gospel tells us that "when his disciples saw it, they had indignation, saying, To what purpose is this waste?" They were provoked. Mark in his Gospel limits the critics by saying that "there were some that had indignation within themselves, and said, Why was this waste of the ointment made?" John puts his finger on the main critic and says it was Judas who raised the storm of opposition: "Why was not this ointment sold for three hundred pence, and given to the poor? " Judas was sure he could have administered the gift better than Mary. He would have spent the money on the poor. He was indignant and spoke in terms of emphatic denunciation. It was a reflection upon Mary. Yes, and upon Jesus.

Why should we have paintings and beautiful churches and adorn the sanctuary of God and spend money on flowers for the sick and the dead and the living, when little children are hungry and people all over the world are dying without the gospel? Why should we ride in limousines, when crippled folk find it hard to walk? Why load the casket with costly flowers, when the poor are knocking at our door? It is an old question. Why was not this ointment sold and the money given to the poor?

The argument is a shattering one. It silences us. Certainly we do not want to see the poor starve, but then the question presses in upon us, Where shall we stop? If the argument is sound, then this very feast in the home of Simon, which Judas and the other disciples were evidently enjoying, would have had to be called off. But let us ask, first of all, Who are the poor? Are we poor simply because we have no bread to eat? Is poverty confined to hunger that finds satisfaction only from a kitchen? Was Jesus hungry? Was he poor? Was he crying out, facing death and the cross, for something that Mary was trying to supply? There is another poverty than that which can be fed by bread. For what are you hungry? All of us are hungry for something. We too belong to the poor. What is it that we need? What would we like to have? Is it not something that will make you feel as if somebody needs you, that somebody believes in you; and are you not satisfied when somebody pours out upon you the wealth of an affection that is dearer to you than all the bakeries or harvest fields in the world?

Furthermore, if it is Judas that is making the complaint, we would not want to take our place beside him. John the apostle did not trust him, and we do not trust him. Judas was not sincere. He was a thief. He was greedy. He wanted to use Mary's gift for himself. We have seen the same thought expressed by many church people. If someone is moved by the goodness of God and the greatness of the gospel to give to foreign missions, others will say, "Why not give it to national missions?" Why give to the heathen abroad; are there not enough heathen at home? If you run down the argument, you will find that it is not the folk who give liberally to national missions who object to foreign missions. The reason lies deeper, within a grudging heart that would keep back part of the price for a selfish purpose.

Notice, also, that it was Mary's gift that Judas wanted to spend. He said nothing about giving his own money to the poor. He was using Mary's sacrifice, not his own. There was once a boy who spent all his Christmas money — seven dollars — for yellow roses for his mother. There is no one who could not have helped that boy to spend his money to better advantage. But, you see, it was his money, and if he wanted to pour out an extravagance of affection for his mother, that was his business and not yours or mine. If a woman wants to be extravagant for her love of Christ, it becomes miserly men to be silent. There are more ways of giving to the poor than by giving bread to the hungry. Charity is not always bound up in bags of flour. Life is more than meat, and the body is more than raiment. The poet, the painter, the musician can all try to make the world more beautiful as well as the philanthropist, the physician, and the preacher.

Something else needs to be said. If Judas and the disciples wanted to give to the poor, there was plenty of opportunity. Jesus made the statement that the poor are always with us, and I imagine that much as we desire to abolish poverty, that condition will always be true. And who, among that crowd of guests, do you imagine was the greatest lover of the poor? Was it Mary, or Judas, or the disciples? This much is certain: The person who pours out treasures for Christ's sake is not likely to be hardhearted or forgetful when the time of need comes. She who breaks alabaster jars for Christ knows more about the poor than all the indignant voices that cry aloud in protest.

No, we are against Judas. We want to be on the side of Jesus. It was Judas who was wrong. Jesus was right. Jesus would not ignore the poor. He would not neglect the needy. He it was who told about the good Samaritan. Jesus was on the side of the poor, but he was against Judas. Jesus took his place with Mary, and, lifting his voice above the troubled murmurings of the crowd, he said: "Let her alone. She has done a beautiful thing. She has done all that she knew how to do. I tell you truly, wherever the gospel is preached, men will speak of what she has done in memory of her."

What a memorial Mary raised that day! She was the only one who understood and entered into our Lord's experience with sympathy and understanding. She knew the meaning of the way he was to take; and before another Sabbath came round, it would be too late to say or to do anything for him. Robert Burns, the Scottish poet, belonged to the great group of hungry, impoverished, and breaking hearts. After his death, when a memorial of hewn stone was erected to him, one of his friends said, "He asked of his generation bread and when he was dead they gave him a stone." If there is something you want to say, something you want to do, any kindness you want to express, any flowers you want to give, do not wait until the door is closed and it is too late.

What memorial have you? Mary has her memorial erected out of an extravagance of love. What extravagance of giving has the love of Christ called forth in you? How are you going to match the extravagance of his love? How will you match his love which poured itself out for you? It is not a question of budgets and subscriptions and quotas. It is a matter of love. Blessed be extravagance! "Our Lord Jesus Christ, though he was rich, yet for your sakes he became poor, that ye through his poverty might be rich." How will you match that? "The Son of man came not to be ministered unto, but to minister, and to give his life a ransom for many." How will you match that? There was nothing beautiful about the cross. It was an instrument of death. It was stained with blood, but Mary wove around it the fragrance of her love and Jesus was satisfied. How will you match the extravagance of such sacrifice?

One of the interesting things that one sees at a wedding are the gifts, and someone who knows the secret behind each one will say: "Mrs. So-and-So gave that. Mr. So-and-So gave that. The mayor of the city gave that. A celebrated judge gave that." It is all sweet and lovely. I wonder what treasures Christ holds in his keeping. Perhaps someday he will show them to us, and he will say, "The widow in the Temple gave this"; and there will be the two mites that were her whole living. "The Samaritan woman gave me that. And the women who came to the tomb on Easter morning gave these spices and fine linen." And around the treasures of heaven will be baskets of flowers, given by the lepers, the lame, and the blind. But among all the memorials that the Master will have to show will be Mary's alabaster jar, still broken and the fragrance of it still filling earth and heaven. And then he will turn to ask, "I wonder what I have of yours?"

32

The Foreign Mission of the Church

"For though I preach the gospel, I have nothing to glory of: for necessity is laid upon me; yea, woe is unto me, if I preach not the gospel!" — I Cor. 9:16.

AMERICA cannot be bounded by any physical lines of latitude or longitude. The ideas and ideals that are born and have their habitation in America do not ask permission to pass through any customhouse in the world. Trade and commerce do not wait until diplomats are satisfied as to what goods should be bartered. The passion for education leaps all obstacles and erects its institutions on the banks of the Nile and on the shores of the Pacific. The glory of the medical profession is that it knows no barriers of race, religion, or nationality, and finds its way to establish clinics and hospitals in cities or villages that still listen to the rhythmic music of the tom-tom. "The moral boundaries of nations no longer match necessarily with their political and physical boundaries." So said a world-renowned statesman. And we say, "It is well."

But what about religion? Have we the same angle on religion that we have on potatoes, beans, oil, tobacco, and pickles? We have a sense of pride that we can export our goods, our books, our steel, our meat, our fruit, our culture. Do we feel the same way about religion? Have we any religion to export? Perhaps you say we need all the religion that we can produce right here. Yes, and perhaps we need all the education, the culture, and medical science right here at home.

Here was a man, for example, whose name was Paul, who was born of an intense nationalism. How did he feel about it? He tells how he felt. He felt that exporting religion was the greatest business of his life, and if he were here today, he would say that automobiles and engines and steel products and the by-products of coal and aluminum and gymnasiums and colleges and psychology are poor things indeed to send out in comparison with religion. Paul was a Jew — a Hebrew of the Hebrews, he tells us; and yet he said, "Necessity is laid upon me; yea, woe is unto me, if I preach not the gospel!" Then he went on to say, in the same passionate eloquence: "I have a stewardship intrusted to me. . . . Though I was free from all men, I brought myself under bondage to all, that I might gain the more. And to the Jews I became as a Jew, that I might gain Jews. . . . To the weak I became weak, that I might gain the weak: I am become all things to all men, that I may by all means save some [A.S.V.]."

Religion is either everything or it is nothing. It is either first or it is nowhere. It is either the best thing in the world or the worst thing in the world, as has been suggested by the Soviet Government, which holds that religion is "the opiate of the people." Paul felt that religion was everything, and so necessity was laid upon him to give his religion universality. Why did he feel that way? Was he eccentric? Was he a fanatic? He was all these, but he was also a man of intellect who could measure words by sacrifice.

First, Paul was aware of *the necessity of a priceless possession.*

He felt that way because he looked upon his religion as something unique and priceless. He had something other people did not have and he was restless to share it with them. He knew something other people did not know and he was impatient to tell them. He knew a secret about God. All over the world men talked about God, but they were not sure. They argued and debated. They erected altars and offered sacrifices. They differed as to the time when God should be worshiped. They disagreed as to God's name and his nature. Dr. Jowett, the Master of Balliol, was once asked by a young inquiring student what he thought about God. Doctor Jowett replied, "That is very unimportant; all that matters is what God thinks about me." What others think about God is interesting, but the big question of importance is, "What does God think of us?"

Paul knew. He was sure. He knew what God thought about the world and the people who live in it. Paul knew this because of what he knew about Jesus Christ. The sinless life of Jesus, his conscience-compelling teaching, his death on the cross, his resurrection into living power made Paul feel certain that he knew something about God that others had not yet learned. From the gospel of Jesus Christ, Paul learned about what God thought of man. This gospel Paul wished to share with all men everywhere. It was a priceless treasure. Because of it Paul was inspired to travel over land and sea to bring to the world the fact that there was reconciliation with God through his eternal love made known in Jesus Christ.

Secondly, Paul was aware of *the necessity of an unsatisfied need.* On all sides the hunger of the world was evident. Paul saw it. We see it. Paul could not get away from it. We cannot get away from it. People wanted to know. People wanted to be sure. People wanted to be fed. In the streets of Athens, Paul found an altar with an inscription, "To the Unknown God." The pity, the tragedy, of it made an eloquent appeal. It was a revelation of a religious hunger that found no satisfaction in philosophers' dreams or politicians' promises. And the truth of it still remains.

The world is filled with altars where we burn incense to the gods we cannot name. Even in this high-living, scientific-thinking land of America innumerable altars are burning to strange gods. Outside America in Europe many bright-colored fires are burning to gods of weird and fierce design. In the Orient and the Middle East men and women are eating their hearts out for gods that neither know them nor care. Across the face of the globe their hunger speaks words of anguish and of torment. We read that in the midst of the modern progress and almost primeval superstition of the South American countries there is a feeling out after something to satisfy and people are burning incense upon the altar of secularism. Everywhere the hungry people look up and are not fed. Once more we learn that man cannot live by bread alone, and if the soul is starved, there is tragedy. Paul knew the need of the heart of the world. Do we know it? Are we so blind as to think that the peoples of the earth will be satisfied with radios and automobiles and farm machinery and electrical appliances? It is still true that the heart was made for God and is restless until it finds its rest in him.

"My faith burns low, my hope burns low,
Only my heart's desire cries out in me;
By the deep thunder of its want and woe
Cries out to Thee."

Thirdly, Paul was aware of *the necessity of unparalleled success*. Paul was not a raw recruit. He had tasted success. What he was saying was the result of mature conviction. He had had twenty years of Christian life. He had had ten years at least of aggressive missionary service. He had been over the ground. He had tramped the hills of Asia Minor and traveled the high seas. He knew the difficulties. He had suffered for his faith. He had known shipwreck, imprisonment, stoning, insult. But he had seen the victory. He had seen the gospel at work. He had firsthand evidence of success, and he was impatient to be out and at work with his missionary evangelism.

In his letters Paul draws the contrast again and again between what men were before the gospel came to them and what they became afterward. Here is one striking parallel: "Be not deceived: neither fornicators, nor idolaters, nor adulterers, nor effeminate, . . . nor thieves, nor covetous, nor drunkards, nor revilers, nor extortioners, shall inherit the kingdom of God. And such were some of you." That is one side of the picture. Here is another side: "But ye are washed, but ye are sanctified, but ye are justified in the name of the Lord Jesus, and by the Spirit of our God."

These contrasts are multiplied since those faraway days. Every photograph of a mission school is eloquent in such contrast. Every mission station, every Christian home, every little Christian child in Korea, in Japan, in India, presents just such a picture. There rises before my vision a picture of the Christian families living over against the pagan life of the Orient. I can close my eyes and see in a little Japanese church father and mother and three Japanese girls all dressed in spotless garments, hymnbook in hand, the light of God in their faces, singing of the Christ who threw open the gate of new life to them. From the Philippines, Thailand, Korea, India, the testimony is the same. "No religion, native or imported — except Christianity — has ever given men and women the place of a person." Thus, the necessity is laid upon us to preach the gospel; for it is still the power of God unto salvation.

> "Far, far away, like bells at evening pealing,
> The voice of Jesus sounds o'er land and sea,
> And laden souls by thousands, meekly stealing,
> Kind Shepherd, turn their weary steps to Thee."

Fourthly, Paul was aware of *the necessity of the preservation of personality*. There is such a thing as the disintegration of personality. Having the truth, knowing the need, seeing the victory, if we refuse to answer the call, there is no longer any haven of salvation, of honor, of duty, of right. I think this was what was in Paul's mind when he said, "Necessity is laid upon me, . . . woe is unto me, if I preach not the gospel!" To save himself he must go forth and fulfill his obligation.

It was by coming back from his long flight into the wilderness and facing Jezebel that Elijah won his right to have a soul. It was by his return from an experience out in the sea and facing the duty that called him to Nineveh that Jonah was saved from moral disaster. It is by losing life that we save it. The church that withdraws into the comfort of its own luxury is dead. The Christian who knows Christ and his power to meet the world's needs and withholds his hand is more than a traitor. To save himself and keep himself from disintegration Paul could not escape the necessity that was laid upon him. He would lose his soul if he did not move out into the path of duty. He would slip from his high place of being a Christian personality and become, like Judas, a traitor whose only destiny was to go out alone into the night and hang himself.

This was Paul's argument. This is what he meant. And if you will follow through his words, you will see how passionately the necessity burned in his soul. "And this I do for the gospel's sake, that I might be partaker thereof with you. . . . I therefore so run, not as uncertainly; so fight I, not as one that beateth the air: but I keep under my body, and bring it into subjection: lest that by any means, when I have preached to others, I myself should be a castaway." Think of the tragedy: All the while the gospel going on and on and on to victory, and I myself a castaway! The moment the Church and the Christian turn their back upon the missionary enterprise that very moment darkness covers the earth.